Growing Up in Old Age

Novels by Margaret Freydberg

The Bride
(1952)

The Lovely April
(1955)

Winter Concert
(1985)

Katherine's House
(1986)

The Consequences of Loving Syra
(1990)

Growing Up in Old Age

Margaret Howe Freydberg

PARNASSUS IMPRINTS
Hyannis, Massachusetts

First Edition

ISBN 0-940160-75-7

Parnassus Imprints, Inc.
30 Perseverance Way
Hyannis, MA 02601

Production supervised by Jenna Dixon

The text of this book is set in 11/14 Adobe Sabon.

Cataloging-in-Publication Data
Freydberg, Margaret Howe.
Growing up in old age / Margaret Howe Freydberg. — 1st ed.
p. cm.
Includes bibliographical references.

1. Freydberg, Margaret Howe. 2. Aging—Psychological aspects.
3. Women authors, American—20th century—Biography. I. Title.

PS3556.R448Z468 1998 813'.54 [B]
QBI97-41127

Manufactured in the United States of America

For Nick

What Are Years?

What is our innocence,
what is our guilt? All are
naked, none is safe. And whence
is courage: the unanswered question,
the resolute doubt,—
dumbly calling, deafly listening—that
in misfortune, even death,
encourages others
and in its defeat, stirs

the soul to be strong? He
sees deep and is glad, who
accedes to mortality
and in his imprisonment rises
upon himself as
the sea in a chasm, struggling to be
free and unable to be,
in its surrendering
finds its continuing.

So he who strongly feels,
behaves. The very bird,
grown taller as he sings, steels
his form straight up. Though he is captive,
his mighty singing
says, satisfaction is a lowly
thing, how pure a thing is joy.
This is mortality,
this is eternity.

—Marianne Moore

Contents

Illustrations

Preface

THE WRITING of this book was begun three years ago, as a search within myself to understand and expectantly to lessen my fears of growing old and to sustain the joy of living I have never been without. The finishing of it was dependent upon the success of my search.

Writing is my chief, conscious way of finding out what I didn't know I knew, of bringing together observations, information and experience stored up in me and processed in there and often delivered eventually as discovery.

And so, when I began this book, I knew that I was writing it primarily for myself and that its first function was to help *me*. But also, at the back of my mind was the idea that even though my fears might be greater than other people's, if I found ways to disempower mine and face old age with reasonableness and courage, those ways might help other aging people do the same, even though the nature of their fears might be different from mine. Because I absolutely believe that fear of old age, no matter what its measure, is fundamentally universal and as old as history, and that all human beings, except those for whom life has become intolerable, are fearful on some level and in some degree about its possible even predictable adversities, and the final exit no one is exempt from. To be alive is to be anxious, beginning with the newborn baby's first cry. So how could aging people not have normal or even abnormal anxieties about being sick and sad and peripheral and, underneath all that, about dying?

As I came upon ways to understand and to tackle my fears, I grew convinced that I was on to something that, since it had already begun to benefit me, could perhaps benefit others; though they might find discrepancies between their fears and mine, they might see that the ways I found to strike at the roots of mine could be applicable to the varieties and gradations of their own.

I found out, too, that the discoveries that led me on and on and are still, open-endedly, leading me on could be helpful not only to aging people but to people of any age. I was tempted to use as a subtitle *A Philosophy of Aging*. But my granddaughter said, "The manner in which you present the 'idea' of aging in the context of your whole life opens that idea up to all people, of any age, to relate to."

And so I decided to use a single title, *Growing Up in Old Age*. For I realized that the philosophy, or "idea," of aging I had arrived at is really a philosophy for the whole span of a lifetime, from its beginning to its ending. If I had known it and followed it years ago, I would have begun to grow up then, rather than now.

It would be a mistake to say that I have entirely succeeded in what I set out to do. But it would be an even greater mistake to say that I have failed. In one sense, the book is finished, in that I have found a means of acknowledging and facing the forces and stratagems of my fears and have begun to take steps to outmaneuver and to outlaw them. But in another sense the book is unfinished and will remain so because I have learned the nature of search and that it never ends.

1 The Foreign Country of Old Age

IT IS the month of may here on this island in the sea. Beach plum is blossoming in white, cloudlike masses along the roads and in the fields.

But I find, when I stop to look closely, that the hearts of the flowerets that make up the clusters of beach plum are a very pale pink, something I wouldn't have realized seeing them from a distance as large, overall white shrubs.

This could be a metaphor for the exploration I hope to do. I must look attentively; look at the particular rather than the general; find the center, which will be a surprise. In the core of everything is the truth of it.

I will begin with what I already know about growing old.

I know that growing old is like finding yourself, surprisingly and disturbingly, in a country that is foreign to you and at an age when your capacities for adaptation to foreignness are diminished.

Suddenly you realize that you are here, in a strange place, and that here you will, without any way of going back, be staying.

In retrospect, you see that it has been a gradual moving away from the place where you have lived familiarly and securely, at first through suburbs that are slightly but not completely unfamiliar, and then, soon, into an open countryside where there are no familiar landmarks at all. In the distance you see the beginnings of a dark forest that stretches as far as the eye can see.

The weather has begun to be different, too, in this foreign place. You are not acclimatizing yourself. You haven't brought the right clothes. In your metaphorical luggage you have clothes that were right for back there where you came from but are not suitable for this place at all.

The food is different, too. Oh, very specifically different. Here there are no croissants, no crusty chicken skin, no pecan pies, and no salt to make your unbuttered vegetables taste the way they did back there.

And the language—well, among other differences, it becomes very, very medical. "Waiting for the results of tests," is a cliché of your days. And "medication." You try to get back to the good old-fashioned word "medicine," hoping that it will restore something you stood for back there, but eventually you give up and go along with everyone else in this place who says "medication." Hearing yourself say it, you wonder why you have allowed yourself to adapt to this jargon. You make a point of thinking that if only you could stick to saying "medicine" you would have somehow challenged all this inexorable unfamiliarity.

You have begun to feel at a loss with almost everything. There are no signposts. And there are pitfalls. You suspect there might even be undetonated land mines here and there. And yes, you find to your terror that there are such booby traps—sudden, explosive, even sometimes disastrous. This is scary, this place. Going cautiously, apprehensively along, you want terribly to be back in that place you knew, where at least life, though not always pleasant and easy, was predictable in its scenery and climate and clothes and food and language.

As you stand alone on this barren plain, your single shadow lying long and black across its late afternoon light, you realize that this new country is bleak and it is lonely, and is without reference to anything you have ever known.

Nothing much terrible has happened to you yet, just little things. But terrible things are happening all the time to others and may happen to you too.

You are at last, admittedly, full of fear.

"Loss" is a word you are now acknowledging. There are little losses, like the inevitability of not finding eyeglasses and car keys. But there are bigger and far more penetrating losses—people who matter to you die, or the work you lived by, and the money you earned from it, you no longer have. Incredulously, you begin to wonder whether, by some immutable process beyond your control, you must now be known to yourself, and to others, as—obsolete?

And there is one very big and unacceptable loss, accelerating irreversibly no matter how much and in what ways you try to slow it down or reverse it—and that is the loss of your looks. It is going, that reinforcing appearance of invincible youth; it is giving way to the rude, real statement of disintegration.

Gone is the reliable, familiar appearance of looking, if not young, then at least not old, of youth grown not-yet-threateningly into middle age. You have lost, and now you see the unkind truth, that reinforcing appearance of youth that has always felt indisputably permanent and that you now realize is not.

Hand in hand with the loss of your looks, in a less obvious but fundamentally more threatening way, comes the loss of what you took back there to be the reliable base of your existence—your self-identity. You call it that now, although you may not have called it that back there, knowing that fulcrum of your existence only as a sense of ongoing self-sameness.

Alas, the self-sameness you had back there in that solid-based-because-familiar and, you felt, immortal place of youth grown into middle age, has begun to feel not reliable at all, even for back there, else it would have *stayed,* like your breathing. It would have been something as unchangeable as, say, your soul. You now see your old self-identity for what it was—an unreliable self-sameness based on the spurious expectations of being perennially young, or middle-aged, based on your then not-very-seriously-changing looks, based on the job you held that you are now retired from, based on whatever role or roles you took to be your signature.

Multiple losses, they call it in this foreign country.

One night I had a dream. Simplistic it was. So simplistic as not to be credible. But believe me, I had it, just as I have sometimes had equally bald dreams that waste no time and employ no surrealism in putting a finger exactly on what, as they say, "the problem is."

I was in a car. I was driving. I was alone. Headlights on. But everything was getting darker. Finally, it was too dark, too impenetrably dark, to see the road in front of me, to see anything at all. I was concerned and said aloud to myself in the dream, "I can't see anything!"

Yet in a minute, I saw the lights of a town ahead—

greenish lights interspersed in the black darkness. Then I was at an inn, a very crowded, popular place, evidently. A woman behind the desk was being besieged by people. Finally she turned to me. I asked for a room and was told that there was not a room to be had. She recommended I try other hotels, though they were expensive, she warned.

Oh dear. I turned away, discouraged. How could I find those other hotels? Then I noticed that a woman applying for a room, and apparently getting one, was handing a passport to the woman behind the desk.

Passport! You needed a passport here?

Naturally, I was in a foreign country. I needed a passport.

But I didn't have mine with me!

Oh, I could so easily have put it in my purse. If only I'd known. If only I'd realized!

And of course now I couldn't go to those other hotels, because they too would demand my passport.

So, I am alone, without a passport, in a foreign country, with no place to lay my head and with headlights that are not serviceable in the threatening dark night of this unfamiliar place.

I feel a fear that is black, like the night.

The puzzling contradiction in many aging people is that they are old, and they look old, but their spirits don't feel old. They can't find anything in their spirits that matches the concept of oldness. In spite of the tremulous hand, the hesitant foot, their emotions are intense, their minds race on and on, their appetites, though less sharp, nevertheless exist. In other words, if a lively spirit, intense emotions, and fervid mind are youthful, then what they feel themselves to be is young.

But when they look in the mirror, they see all this inner youth as improbable, as some illicit self that hasn't learned to behave, cavorting away in there behind this depressing facade of wrinkles and pouches that has taken on, it seems to them, a kind of stern, implacable maturity.

How do I reconcile these somehow opposing forces of the inner *feelings* with the *fact* of old age? And how do I find anything to call self-sameness in that oppositional persona I see in the mirror? Was my self-sameness, back there, mostly my looks? Was I, perchance, mostly my face, and my smooth belly, and my firm upper arms? To what woman does this aging face—with the turkey wattles under the chin that are getting more and more pendulous—belong? Does it now belong to someone other than the woman whose face was once unlined, whose underchin was smooth as a right angle, whose arms were solid as a sculpture?

If there is an inner woman there, other than the woman I see in the mirror, who is she?

Until this question is answered (if it can be), I will continue to look in the mirror and then look quickly away, pretending that what I see is not so, forgetting that it is so as I go about my day in which, metaphorically speaking, there are no mirrors.

Possibly fear of a fading face is worse for me, who was born with a pretty one, than for women who were not. I have been concerned all my life with my looks. (And I bring this up because that preoccupation with attractiveness is not only relative to but also to a great extent the cause of the problems I am encountering in my old age.) My looks have played, prominently, a determining role in the development, or should I say retardation, of my life. My looks have been my self-identity, my means whereby. In my childhood, I learned that I could get where I thought I wanted to go by my appearance alone. My appearance seemed to me to be the passport to everything I thought I wanted. (Passport?) For a long time, my attractiveness was my success story. I had, I thought, no other bait but that. I grew so used to being regarded in a certain way that eventually I came almost entirely to depend upon it.

Why, then, when I was a very little girl, did I burst into tears one day on a streetcar with my brother, when a man sitting beside me turned and ran a finger through one of my curls while saying something tender? Perhaps the dependency on such male attentiveness had not yet begun, and the tiny girl's tiny emergent soul cried out, literally, against what must have seemed a violation of something essential to her. Was she already asking, "To whom do my curls belong?"

Another feeling, one that I know is absolutely unreasonable and that I am increasingly uncomfortable with these days, is how I view old age in others. I am ashamed of how I react to them, even how I shrink from them, I suppose because I am loath to identify with them.

I know that a part of this is an indoctrinated commitment to the cult of female youth that every slick magazine cover in the world sells so predictably and so monotonously—slim, aerobic-ed young body; fresh, pretty, clear-eyed young face; perfect round young breasts revealed through cleavage, oh breasts and breasts and breasts.

But I have more profound reasons for disliking the unlovely signs of old age. From some source I would like to disavow, I condemn old age. I look on the faces of the old and pity what I see, which strikes me as wreckage—not wrinkles in faces so much as sagging flesh under the chin. I look at this with repugnance and think that it is the ultimate demeaning of human form, its helpless debasement.

Do the young in our society, and even the middle-aged, feel this way about old people? Do the young look at me with pity, do they shrink away from me as I shrink away from wrinkles and wigs and walkers? And do they think, or feel, "Ah, I am young. I have everything that that implies. And you, poor old woman, are old. You have lost your looks, you are slow, you are fuddled, you keep dropping things, forgetting where you put things, your loose throat wobbles when you talk. You have lost your importance. You are not important at all now, because you have grown old. It is I, the young woman, who am important now, because I am so wonderfully, desirably young. You are no longer on top, you are underneath, in fact, you are at the bottom. You are negligible, you are nothing. Of course, if I am a generous, kind, or even sensitive young woman, I feel sorry for you. Or if you have some particular wisdom that moves me and inspires me, I will look at you in a different way. Yet I will continue to think that the loose and quivering folds of your neck are unlovely and make you very, very inferior. And the way you struggle up and out of a car, panting, makes you someone I'm glad I am not. The way you mutter, 'Oh, that memory of mine,' gives me a lift because I am not old and senile like you."

Is this the way the young or middle-aged view the unbeautiful elderly? Or is it only that this is the way *I* feel about them, without, of course, the salvation of feeling myself to be young and superior?

Even though my feelings about old people are unreasonable and negative, I also have reasonable and positive thoughts about old people. I know, for instance, that an old face can have an attractive spirit. Yes, I really do know that. The spirit has gentled its intent, the learning about life and the acceptance of it have given it a soft light. What I see in a face like that is, yes, enviable. It is wisdom. I think I could call it beauty. And usually with it, I see a dignity that makes absurd any criticism of the slow and wasted body below it.

I really do know, underneath my emotions of repugnance, that old women like myself no doubt feel as inwardly young as I feel. And also that every old woman feels, thinks, acts in a way unique to her, for she is the only one of her kind on this earth. Her spirit is uniquely hers. Her body is not. She was given that, born with it, for better or for worse. But she herself has made her spirit. Of course, she has been given some of its essence genetically, but the nurturance of it, the making or breaking of it, has been her own work, her own doing.

And so reason tells me that it is my spirit that is essential to me now, because it is all I have that is truly of my own making. And therefore spirit, not body, should be the thing that merits my attention in any other old person, or deserves comment. I don't have to say of some old woman, "I cannot like your wrinkles and your pouches and your lameness, which no one could possibly claim are attractive, but if you have an inner something that attracts me, I can like that. I can see that your spirit is what you are, and what you have basically always been, and that your wrinkles and your pouches and your lameness are not the part of you that needs to matter now."

Reason also tells me that old age must be looked at

without comparison to youth, for how can a progression from birth to death, which is growth, be viewed with any logic comparatively? The progression of one life is a single thing, one life in motion, and any valid comparison would have to be of two lives of the same age in motion, or of one life at different stages, or of two lives at different stages. And what use is comparison anyway?

What is emerging in me is an ambivalence between the unreasonableness of my negative feelings about the looks of old age and the reasonableness of my positive realization that such a point of view is not serviceable now and never was.

Good. Even as I write, a growing reasonableness has begun to tackle the dilemma. And I tell myself that I must see something in the mirror besides my wrinkled veneer if I am to have any calm; that I will have to make my peace with the loss of smooth skin, and find satisfaction in the gaining of something to take its place. Something, yes, that should always have been in me. Or something that has always been in me but has never seen the light of day.

And so I stand in this open countryside where there are no familiar landmarks, and it comes to me suddenly that, yes, this is the country of old age.

I am old. What's more, I accept the reality, humbling though the thought is, that people will look at me and see that I am old.

It has gone, that mindless safety, so blissful while it lasted, of believing that it couldn't happen to me. It has gone. And I feel strangely different, if empty.

I am old. I seem to have faced a fact.

Perhaps this is the moment at which, in this new and strange country, as my past self-regard is uselessly struggling to maintain itself, and a part of me is still not wanting to believe that this peculiar metamorphosis of aging is actually happening to me, perhaps nevertheless this is the second at which acceptance has finally arrived. This *is* the country of old age.

I am in it. And I fear it.

I have taken the first big step.

2 Am I to Spend the Rest of My Life in the Fear of Losing It?

I AM in my tent, with a quail calling through the daisies in front of it. This tent, my writing place for the warm months of the year, is set in a back field that spreads above the patio behind the house, where the web of a great willow tree that shades it sways in the constant winds from the sea.

The sun has all at once taken the place of early morning fog. Now all is bright. The mood of the earth is suddenly altered, and for a moment, so is mine.

And finding, in terms of ongoing good fortune, the perfection of sitting down to write in this tent with flaps on three sides open to the field, I pick up my pencil ready to tackle the subject of FEAR, which is what I am setting out to understand through the writing of this book. What a contradiction it is to be enraptured with daisies and quail and at the same time to know that I have in me a fear that can make all this unseeable.

So. Where to begin?

In a sudden diversionary tactic, I fill a paper cup with water from my thermos and begin to sip it blankly.

There is a sound that is not quail. I look up. Nick stands in the opening of my tent. My husband Nick. He doesn't like to disturb me when I'm writing and now apologizes for thinking he is doing so. But he isn't, really. I love the surprise of seeing him suddenly there, and the distraction from having to apply myself to fear. He has come to tell me that Rebecca is on the phone saying that the Relaxation group is called off for today and can it be tomorrow at four? It's okay with the others if it is with me.

I tell him that it's okay. And then, "I wish you wouldn't go," I say. "I wish you'd stay. Sit down and listen to the quail."

"Rebecca's waiting on the phone. And anyway, you're supposed to be working."

Yes. I'm supposed to be working. I'm supposed to be thinking about fear.

And so he departs, my husband Nick.

I wonder what *he* feels inside about being old?

It occurs to me that in starting to explore fear, I should begin with Nick, because he is the center of my life, and my happiness seems in a profound and complex way to be dependent on him and on our life together, and this happiness now seems threatened by our old age.

Nick is a mysterious man. He is quiet, reticent (even taciturn), private (yet accessible), instinctively charming, but only when he wants to be; silent when he wants to be; even unpleasant when he wants to be. He is sophisticated and passionate at the same time. He is honorable, he is fastidious. He thinks deeply and continuously. He is shy (though he says he is not). This shyness can often be taken for rudeness, indeed, that is what it looks like. He can be indifferent, which is also taken as rudeness but is, in fact, a lack of interest in the person. The people he is interested in, and who come to him for advice, are rewarded by a penetrating commonsense wisdom that in some cases has altered the course of their lives. There are young men to whom he is a surrogate father. He is quite purely nonjudgmental. But he is immovably unforgiving. (Unlike me. I am judgmental but forgiving). He likes it that I am forgiving. I can see that he thinks of my forgivingness with regard. His mouth is simple as a child's, smooth and pink with health, equable and sweetly curved, taking what comes. He loves dogs, but he loves cats more. The tenderness of his hand stroking a cat's back has a delicacy that is voluptuous. One always remarks his many-layered gentleness, which seems particularly evident because it seems so contradictory to his iron-muscled masculinity. He doesn't know himself, I believe, anywhere near as well as he thinks he does. And yet his personal and intellectual honesty is unwavering. He has a reverence for good wines. And a fascination with foreign cars. He, like my father, hasn't a trace of pretentiousness. He is strong as an ox but has been bludgeoned with terrible operation after terrible operation, which have done their work of wearing him out.

He does not appear to fight "what is," but if he does, he never speaks of it. He is enigmatic (one of the reasons he fascinates me). But I think perhaps he is quiet because he feels no need to say all that he knows. And so it follows, of course, that *I* do not know, and will never know, what goes on in him deeply about the decline of his life.

So far, I do know this much about facing the challenge of old age: One has to make a certain peace with the conditions of it. And I see that Nick has. He is sensible and strong enough to accept reality and to deal with it, and for that reason, I don't think he feels visceral fear as I do. But at some level I know he is not at peace with his life now; in fact, I think he is very sad about it and, of course, bored with it.

I know he *knows* that he is old, because he says from time to time, "I'm getting old," in a dignified, quiet, fatalistic way that is nevertheless loud with implications. But I am fairly certain, knowing as much of Nick as I do, that fear does not ever lie like a stagnant pool at the bottom of his stomach as it often does in mine.

The funny thing is that I refuse to acknowledge the truth, the fact, of what he is declaring. Even though we are both the same age (just a year apart), and even though I have finally accepted the fact of my own old age, and though I may see that when he says "I'm getting old" he is trying to convey to me something profound and complex and alarming about his old age, something he needs me to "get," for God's sake—still, I do not "get" it. I refuse to "get" it.

For one thing, he does not seem old to me. And he certainly does not look it. His face is rested and rosy, not much lined; there are no pouches under his eyes and just a minimal sagging under his chin. True, his hair is snow-white, but it began to turn white in his fifties, so I'm used to it. And he walks shufflingly because he is chronically tired and because his legs are stiff and underexercised. And he is an absolute skeleton—weight lost and never regained after two recent operations. Yet with all these signs of aging, I don't think of him, ever, as an old man.

And yet I know I fear old age for him—this old age that is staring me in the face and that I refuse to "get."

I think I have to see and to admit that I don't accept the fact of Nick's being an old man for the reason that *I do not want him to be an old man.*

I am afraid of Nick's being old. Oh yes, bottomlessly, I fear old age for Nick. Which really means that I also fear his old age for myself.

I fear old age for both of us. What will growing old do to Nick's life? And since his life is so much interfused with mine, what will his growing old do to my life?

And finally, what would I do without Nick? What would Nick do without me?

Three years ago, in March, he had a minor stroke. And then in May he had another one, due to his having decided he didn't need the anticoagulant anymore, and so stopped it without telling the doctor or me. "That was very naughty of you, Nicholas," the nurse in the doctor's office rebuked him, but with awe.

Providentially, both strokes were so slight as to leave no visible or audible impairment, except at first a slightly weakened right hand that was soon, through exercises, restored to full strength. No one felt that Nick was impaired in any way; no one, that is, except Nick himself. He felt, in ways he did not try to describe, that he had slowed down irreversibly. And perhaps he *had* slowed down somewhat. But I also suspect that he let each stroke be a stop sign. In any event, to me they seemed to be the abrupt, perhaps even anticipated by him, culmination of the gradual slowing down of mind and body that had been going on for over a year. Even long before the first stroke, he had ceased trying to think up a problem to keep himself occupied. Problem solving has been the thorough and jubilant activity of Nick's life—in his book publishing business, then in his profession of social psychology, and

Nick

finally in the ecologically oriented land development career of his retirement here on the island.

But now that essential involvement is no longer available within himself. And when people ask him what he is involved in at the moment, he says with a certain bitter succinctness, "Nothing. Nothing at all. I'm getting old. Life goes yawn."

You could say that the use of his mind in high gear has been, in a way, his all, but now that has stopped. And so has exercise. He once played a pounding game of squash but gave it up because he began to dislike and distrust the feeling of competition it aroused. Even so, he is an avid watcher of football on television and never misses a Rose Bowl game. (Man, you are a contradiction!) He was an oarsman and a sailor and a hiker, but lack of vigor and mobility has put an end to all that. Last year he sold his beloved schooner, *Daughter of Dove*, because he couldn't do anything on it except sit while others did the sailing.

And so I do see that he has really stopped, has ceased to engage, that some kind of necessary energy and interest have gone. He is frail, he is idle, he is bored. The only interest he appears to have is in reading his three favorite magazines—*The Economist*, *The New York Review of Books*, and *The New Yorker.* But that is all he does—read. Oh, once a day he dutifully and with obvious reluctance takes his twenty-minute walk ploddingly around the deck. But otherwise he sits in his swivel chair in his study, and reads. His life seems to me to be all input: digestion of input, thought about input I'm sure, yet no output. Being an isolate and no lover of formal sociability or, actually, of any sociability, he doesn't go to men's lunch clubs or to lecture programs or to anything of the sort. Retirement programs? Perish the thought! And so, really, he has no one to talk to about what he reads and thinks except me, his wife. And we have never gotten very far, in our forty-seven years of marriage, with a satisfactory or stimulating exchange of what he thinks about and what I think about, for this is not the kind of talk that has ever gone on between us, being as we are so different. After all our years together, I still have not accustomed myself to the reality of Nick and me being incompatible conversationally. I have never stopped longing to have us be intellectual mates, which of course we are not and never will be. I still want us to be in touch where we live most vitally—in our minds—to be close to each other in that important way, as we are close in so many other ways, even though at bottom I know it is not possible for us, for it is mutually understood that his mind is trained and experienced and sharp in a way mine is not. And these days, compassion for his aloneness has intensified my need to do something to help him if I can and for a closeness to him I cannot do without. But my efforts toward talk as a means of closeness usually leave me with a feeling of the two of us being an unfinished couple, and particularly of me being incomplete in relation to him.

I am sure, as perhaps Nick is, that the day he had the first stroke was a turning point in his life, and in mine—the beginning of the road down.

It was such a thunderbolt of an experience that even now, when I put on my tan quilted coat to go somewhere in the car, I have an immediate visceral memory of that telephone call.

I am in my study when the phone rings. It is up to me to answer it, since Nick has taken the truck down to the tire place to have four new tires put on. I am working on my novel *The Magnolia Room*, and impatiently, because my lap is full of papers, I get up and cross the room to pick up the receiver. "Hello."

"Paey . . ."

"Nick. Yes darling?"

"Arnm haeing au efiso . . ."

I knew right away. Everything stood still. Everything ceased except my shocked center connecting with Nick's slurred speech. "Slurred speech," my mind said. "'Episode.' He's trying to say 'episode'!"

"Nick, listen, where are you? Are you at the tire place?"

"Yuas . . . Arnm haeng efiso . . ."

"I'll be right there. I'll leave the instant I can get my coat on."

Everything had been known to me in less than a second. I saw my room and the brown bare lawn beyond the window, and I saw the sea. I saw everything. The moment was one in which everything was revealed in searchlight clarity as having the central meaning: stroke, and all the grim difference that can commence with it. I stood there experiencing the abrupt, bludgeoning alteration of existence.

At the tire place Nick was sitting in the waiting room on a couch. One of the workmen was standing close by, drinking coffee intently and darting furtive, curious looks at Nick, who wanted none of him.

I don't remember what I said or did, except that I was beside Nick instantly. Then I think I started in about getting the ambulance. I think I said, "I'm going to call the ambulance."

"No." And what had just weakened away in him now

suddenly came back full force in another, louder, more furious, "No."

He stood up unsteadily from the couch. Brushed past me, heading feebly and furiously for the door. I followed, trying to urge the ambulance on him, getting shrill, bossy, a little wild, but already knowing that maybe it was safe not to have the ambulance.

He was trying to distance himself from me. He walked not as unsteadily as I would have supposed he would—could this be not a bad stroke?—toward the car while I headed for the driver's side before he could get there, and, oh good, he went sensibly to the passenger side and got in.

"We're going to the emergency, we'll be there in no time," I said hysterically, while trying not to be hysterical. I was trying to pull myself together for his sake, to seem not to be scared.

All the way to the hospital, which is ten minutes from the tire place, he sat straight up, rigid, looking fixedly ahead, silent as stone, contained in what I felt was panic and fury. I wanted him not to be so furious with me. Yet I knew it wasn't me he was furious with. My heart had begun a fast, ugly pounding.

It turned out to be the slightest of strokes. But in spite of our entreaties, the doctor insisted on keeping Nick in the hospital overnight. And when I walked into his room the next morning, having called the nurses' desk early and been told that he was doing well and could go home, there he was all dressed and sitting up in a chair and ready to leave the minute I got there.

"Hello, darling," he said softly, in a wonderfully, perfectly clear, unslurred voice.

I went to him and kissed his cheek. We were both silent for a moment. Then he said quietly, "I'm all right now."

But he was never again entirely all right. From that day on he was contained within a boundary that kept him in it and anyone else out of it.

Three years have gone by since that day. But every time I am alone in the car in my tan quilted coat, driving up the hill from our house, I am, for a second, a coat and a word struggling to be "episode," and a knowledge of an end now in sight.

Fear is not new to me, not something that has suddenly appeared in my old age. I have always been "anxiety prone." Even fifty years ago my first husband and our children called me "Panicky Peggy;" and before I married Nick, he gave me a little jug with these words written on its curving side: "Don't worry, it may never happen." And so now, inevitably I suppose, in this new and foreign country of old age, fear has become an active and pervasive emotion that often disturbs my days and witches my nights.

I am usually first aware of it in my stomach. Someone will begin to talk about illness, or death, or disaster (just let anyone mention the word "stroke"), or I will have a passing thought about something like that, and suddenly, there in my stomach is a sinking feeling, like dread.

I hate it because it is so unassailable. I hate it because it is so unreasonable. I hate it most of all because I know that what I am feeling is not *specifically* a fear of illness, or of aging, or of death, or of any other disasters—although they are all offshoots of the major inclination—but something generalized and less than conscious that goes on in me perpetually, which is an underlying *proneness* to being fearful, the cumulative result of which is the fear of it—the fear of fear.

Now at last, in my old age, I have come to know that this proneness to fear is the major switch that controls all the other switches; that it is behind all the other fears, is the most powerful of all of them, and is clearly the hardest to tackle. And I see that until I come to grips with the nature and the machinations of that immense and controlling tendency, I will not be fully capable of dealing with the specific fears that spread from it. At this point I don't know whether this proneness to fear is a genetic predisposition or whether by now I am so deeply fed up with a lifetime of assorted fears that the single underlying emotion of fear has become greater than its fearing parts.

Because of the tragedy of the family I was born into, I am, literally, a "born worrier." My parents lost their first child, William, who was normal in all respects, in a crib death when he was seventeen days old. Next, my brother Winthrop, a cheerful, courageous, imaginative, talented, humorous fellow whom I dearly loved and who is now dead, was born with a visible and disfiguring congenital eye disease, not severe enough in the early stages to prevent limited sight, but becoming blindness later. Then I came, safe and sound and completely normal. Then came my sister Helen, totally blind of the same genetic disease as my brother's but even more disfigured—a brave person trying hard to make the best of what she had been dealt, a combination of guts and self-abnegation, all wrapped in exquisite courtesy with tumult underneath.

And so, because of these tragedies, apprehension, along with sadness and fear, was the condition and the climate of my home, and I was programmed for scenarios of the worst from the day of my birth (perhaps even in the womb). During my childhood and my adolescence and, cumulatively, with a lot of guilt thrown in, throughout my adulthood, this has been the big story of my life.

The presence of a transfusing stream of love and encouragement from mother to child, as much as the milk of her breasts, is a lifeline.

In the absence of this life-giving transfusion, the child, experiencing the opposite of being given life, absorbs her first sense of death.

And from this early darkness, fear is born.

Once, Mother had put her arms all the way around me and held me for a long time. I was four years old. I had fallen in the lake, kneeling by the water's edge, playing with stones that were wet and slippery. The wave must have come up without my seeing it, because I can't remember it at all. What I can remember is my white Sunday dress, with alternating rows of lace and voile on the skirt—a row of lace, a wide row of voile, a row of lace—scalloped lace edging the bottom of the skirt, and two pink satin knotted ribbon bows at the waist. My white strap pumps got soaked too. The buttons—white with silver pinpoints in the middle—were stiff and hard to push into the slits in the straps. Why hadn't Mother taken off my shoes and socks for the beach? Come to think of it, why was I dressed that way for the beach? Maybe we had been visiting someone at the lake on a Sunday afternoon, and

Mother had left me in my Sunday dress for the visit. My socks were white ribbed silk. How could I have noticed details like that at the age of four, or whatever very young age I was? But I am certain, absolutely certain, that I was dressed that way, because the tragedy of it was getting the dress all wet, and the shoes. I must have been scared as well, but this part I can't recall. I can remember the dress and the golf cape, but I have no memory of the wave or of being scared. Why a "golf" cape? Mother never played golf. But it was Mother's "golf cape," that's what everyone called it, and the tremendously important thing about the golf cape was leaning against Mother in the backseat of the car on the way home, with the golf cape all around me and Mother's arm all the way around me, holding me because I was shivering in my wet clothes under the warmth of the scratchy golf cape. Surely Father was driving, but I can't remember seeing the back of his head. I can only remember being wrapped up in the golf cape and held against Mother all the way home. And Wint was just a blur, just a blur of a little boy on the other side of Mother, whose arms were not around him but were all the way around me.

Mother's eyes were gray—gray as stone, ancient. Young men up and down Oxford Street dropped in to see her, to talk to her, confide in her. Almost everyone confided in Mother, particularly her friends for hours and hours on the telephone, but I did not. I was instinctively and unquestioningly anchored to the being and the behavior of my mother, but it was an anchorage that was like something I wore, something I put on that could be taken off but never would be, not as close to me as my own skin but like a garment I wore next to my skin. In spite of this I did not confide in Mother. It was this subtle but fundamental lack of interfusion that prevented me from confiding in Mother.

Mother always looked at me with an expression of tolerance, of compassion (or was it wistfulness) for one so young, so giddy, so guided by emotions, and so infinitely removed from the tonnage of responsibility for her handicapped children and her secret and volatile husband that burdened her own pragmatic, serious self. When, if ever, would this wild and basically ungovernable girl develop character? Know right from wrong?

Mother was not a toucher, so she never patted Don, our collie. Perhaps she barely noticed him, though in an abstract way she was fond of him. She was fond of dogs and was terrified of cats. And of mice. A mouse in the house, and she screamed. She loved babies. And antiques, and the selection of fabrics to go with them. And the simmering of crab apples on the kitchen stove, giving her household its promise of Mrs. MacDonald's clear, glowing crab apple jelly. And the "luncheons" she went to and gave (she had "a host" of women friends), using her best lace doilies kept flat between circular damask-covered boards in the reproduction Hepplewhite sideboard with its inlay trim, on the top of which was the silver tea and coffee service used on the occasions when she had "teas" and one of her good friends "poured."

God was there, though, underneath all this, and the devout love of him, and the rocklike strength of twenty women. Had she had more imagination and less religiosity, she could have borne better the tragedy of her children. On the other hand, had she had less strength, she couldn't have borne it at all. She was bolstered—determined, too—by a steady, good, pragmatic, even shrewd mind, which had always managed her household and given it its attractiveness and womb comfort, had mapped out the thoroughly excellent education that my sister Helen was having from tutors and that I was having and would continue to have—private lessons in French and in piano, the girls' school I attended run by two old women who demanded one's best (which I never gave to lessons), the top-notch boarding school I would go to and give my best or be expelled, such was the perfection of its academic standard. "Do it with thy might" was the school's slogan, emblazoned on the escutcheons of its paneled corridors.

Ah yes. "Do it with thy might." That was something I did not need to be taught.

I know that I am fearful. I know intimately what fear feels like. But what do I know, if anything, about other people's fears?

I do know what everyone knows: that fear of old age is as old as time, and that I am not the only person who feels it. In fact, I would imagine that I share this unpleasant emotion, more or less, with just about every person on this planet. Certainly the seed of it is in everyone from the moment of birth, and it grows as the years go on, until in old age it becomes more conscious, more specific, more easily imaginable in the ways of suffering, and of dying.

There must be as many variations and degrees of fear of old age, and of dealing with the prospect of it, as there are individuals. I know people who are visibly unstrung by thoughts of the future, who are rattled or perplexed or scared by what old age may have in store for them. I know others who say that they are not afraid at all, but this doesn't mean that they are without fear. "All people are variously vulnerable and strong, variously functional and dysfunctional. . . . But, though everyone is afraid, on some level, of dying, not everyone is *consciously* afraid of dying. Because many people deal with the fear by denial, and by assuming that they will never die—it's always the other person down the block, but never themselves. Since one's own consciousness is the center of the universe, it is unimaginable that that is going to stop. And it is also unbearable. So that many people, even maybe most people, never think about it consciously."[1]

It goes without saying that religion is one way to stave off fears of death. People whose faith promises life after death, though perhaps not entirely able to accept old-age illnesses with resignation, can nevertheless transcend those worries and find some peace in the contemplation of an ending they believe is not a total extinction but only a transition from this life to the next one. "I don't believe in a man in the sky on a throne," says my close friend Letty, "but I know there's *something* out there we don't even begin to comprehend. I *know* we go on. I have absolute faith that we go on."

And I have known many mature and strong irreligious people (like my husband) who deal pluckily with serious problems and who surely adapt better than the less strong to the gradual, unfamiliar, and life-threatening prospects of old age, which is not to say that they aren't fearful of it on some level. I imagine they don't spend their time worrying unduly about what could happen (or don't, like me, read every obituary in the local newspaper whether I knew the person or not), but gear themselves reasonably toward medical prevention of big illnesses and postponement of dying, and take precautions as best they can against the circumstances or dispositions that are likely to make illness and dying premature. I also imagine that in spite of whatever fears they have, they deal practically with the future and courageously with the present.

Demonstrably, they cope. "How are you?" I ask a friend I meet on the street. "Oh, hanging in there," he replies with what is either mock humor or stoicism, lighted by an attempt at cheer.

I do so admire this debonair, seeming mastery of the deep difficulties and afflictions and, presumably, fear that I know this man to have.

Coping implies strength. It implies endurance. It implies a will not to be defeated. "Life must go on." And my friend is somehow managing not to be thoroughly downed by the way life is for him now, or by fears of what is going to become of him. I think this is remarkable and brave.

Actually, when you think of the gallantry of so many people in the face of the multiple losses of old age, it appears that the human spirit is endowed with something to cope with heavy-duty experiences and with fears both imagined and real. For example, look at and listen to a busload of senior trippers unloading at some scenic spot, and the flirtatiousness of three women in pastel pants suits who have fastened onto one of the few single men on the tour. You will be impressed by a spirit of gaiety, adventure, camaraderie, interlaced, of course, with caution. And in your heart you will commend them for putting a good face on what must be, for many of them, an effort to forget their fears and their limitations and their lamenesses and the little bottles of "medications" in their luggage.

As I watch them, with admiration and interest and even with envy, I find myself wondering how old people do it, marveling that any old person can even be *expected* to deal gracefully and positively with the known losses of old age, or even how any one of them can be expected to rally from one strong loss after another in this foreign country where there are no replacements for these kinds of losses.

As I get deeper into the contemplation of fear, I find that it has many careers. One of them is the self-delusion that it is a "preparation" for dealing with calamity. There are those (I among them) who rationalize that by improvising scenarios of all the possible bad things that can happen to them, they are girding themselves to deal with them when they strike. And if doubts about the sanity of this fantasizing underlie it, they reassure themselves that forewarned is forearmed, and that they are simply, in a practical way, getting ready to face, and to deal with, the worst. I suspect that I use the technique of worry-as-preparation to fortify myself against a deep and gripping belief that, unlike my friend the coper, I don't have it in me to deal with calamities at all. I have no confidence that I won't fall apart if something awful happens.

I know, though, that it doesn't work—this prognostic preparation for dealing with disaster. To paint a typical melodramatic sequence of concerns about illness and death, let's say that I am imagining every nuance of a coming visit to the doctor that may reveal cancer, though there is no reason to suspect that this may be so. I go on to imagine the subsequent surgery, the return of the cancer after a year, then the slow, miserable months that end in death, my bereaved husband (who will cook for him?), the memorial service at which my dear friends weep, the music I must select ahead of time (would Brahms's Double

Concerto be too grandiose?), and so forth and so on.

Or another scenario, just as melancholy and, I suspect, quite common: A very old woman (me) is living alone in a small apartment in an elder housing unit. On her bedside table is a rectangular plastic foolproof pill container with seven snap-lid compartments for the seven days of the week; and beside it, a telephone that never rings. She sits in a Barcalounger and rocks slowly, perpetually, back and forth, back and forth, waiting for the sound of the mailman who delivers only catalogues—there is almost never a letter—or for the hearty greeting of the United Parcel man delivering something she has ordered from a catalogue just for the sake of receiving a package and opening it. Or she waits for the lively hour that the young, pretty, cheery home health aide spends once a week, stowing the groceries she has bought in the tiny, under-the-counter refrigerator and in the one little cupboard over it, and tidying up what the old woman can't tidy herself because she can't bend or stoop or lift. The telephone never rings. The lonely old woman never dials it, because she doesn't know anyone to call—the friends she once had in this building have all gone. As she jokes to the home health aide, "Everyone I know is dead." And enveloping everything is the constant crackle and drone of the television that is never turned off. It even goes on all night long if she has fallen asleep while looking at it.

Of course, the fact is that such old-age scenarios can happen pretty much the way I imagine them, and perhaps more often than not, do. And since the older I grow the more my chances of going scot-free decline, you could say that if I wanted to bet on the worst scenario happening, I would win.

However, I am learning something very important as I

go along. It is that even if there is a likelihood of the worst coming to pass as I foresee it, I still cannot be certain that it will. Many, many times in my life there have been serious crises, but none of them ever had any resemblance to my previews of them, and none of them turned out to be as impossible to deal with as I had thought they would be. In other words, trying to prepare myself for them was simply an exercise in futility—hours and hours of wasteful, mind-muddling daydreaming that never turned out to be of any use at all when the time came.

It has been proved to me again and again that in my forebodings of disaster I was never, in imagining a possibility, dealing with a certainty. And so I do know, absolutely, that I cannot prophesy what is going to happen in any future critical situation or how I am going to feel or behave in it. How can I know what innumerable elements a fantasized future situation will be composed of, since the fears I am generating at the moment are based on the experience of past fears, and all experience changes in every moment—in this present moment and in the following moment—so that there is no possible way to predict the moment that follows this one? If, in the 525,600 minutes of the 365 days of the past year alone, I have from minute to minute received an input of always ongoing and slightly different experience, and assimilated all this and processed it innerly to create for the moment alone a unique, never-to-be-repeated experience, how can I possibly predict the emotional and physical content of any minute beyond that minute or hour beyond that hour?

> For the pattern is new in every moment
> And every moment is a new and shocking
> Valuation of all we have been.[2]

And so it is safe to say that if one of the dire scenarios I set up in my imagination comes to pass, it could turn out quite differently from my unrealistic and pessimistic predictions; it is safe to say that none of the scenes—Act One, Act Two, Act Three, Act Four—will happen in the way I imagine it will, and that if the imagined illness or loss does turn out to be a real one, I may find something in me that can confront the threat, something I have had no experience with because heretofore I haven't had to, but still, something held in storage that will come to my rescue, if not immediately, then eventually, simply through the instinctive process of self-preservation.

Another bizarre consequence of ruminations of disaster I have just recently come to understand is that by trying to live through the worst possible imagined situations that can occur, if perchance they do occur, I have managed to make myself live through them twice—once in imagination, once in actuality. Oh, how I waste my time!

Also, even this early in the book, I am already aware that if I indulge in scenarios of the worst (for, yes, I think this is a form of self-indulgence), I am not in any viable way giving myself preparation for facing disaster. Because forewarned is *not* forearmed, but disarmed. All of that forewarning uses up the spirit, dissipates the energies that need to be held together and solidified and stored up for the big uses of the future.

* * *

Am I to spend the remainder of my life in the wasteful grip of the fear of the loss if it?

The answer I give myself is no—a very decided no. Because worry—I mean the unreasonable excess of it that is my heritage—is now absolutely unacceptable to me, and I am sick of it. It is not only a damaging visitation emotionally and a handicap physically (causing psychosomatic ailments and thereby actually shortening the life I am at such pains to prolong) but also a constant threat to those things I long so much to preserve. It is the "suffering [that] is for fools."[3]

I am determined not to let fear deprive me of the happiness that has always come naturally to me, and to find a way to live without being subjected to, or rather without subjecting myself to, an escalating worry about imagined sufferings and endings. How remarkable it would be to live without an overriding worry about how or how long I will remain in this life, to live with interest, with the absorbed passion that has always been the strong pulse of my being in spite of the very real and great difficulties of my life. Somehow I know that the desire for happiness, even though that happiness might eventually be transmuted from known forms into forms I have had no experience with, has to be the way for me to continue in spite of the heavy difficulties and the heavier, darker promises of old age.

With respect, I give the pursuit of making one's peace with death, of learning to accept it as a part of life, its deserved due. I have not explored this philosophic discipline that exists in varying ways in all cultures and religions, because I haven't had any interest in doing so, haven't felt any inclination to. But I do realize, respectfully, that innumerable people have a disposition to accept, during their lives, the reality that they will die. (Some of us unbelievers may even be envious of the security this gives believers.) But that path, I know, is not my way to go. For though I don't "rage, rage against the dying of the light,"[4] I know that to have a joy of living, as well as a considerable contemplation of dying, is for me a contradiction in functions. In a person with a strong life force and a sizable joie de vivre, how can such an energy of being prepare itself to die?

3 Happiness

IT IS as obvious as sun on a clear day that all people on earth, of any age, want to be happy in the ways they know happiness.

People experience happiness in different ways. And so I can only confidently describe happiness if I describe my own kind.

By happiness, I don't mean what could be thought of as conventional high spirits, or even a mindless plateau of pleasure. No. My own happiness—I can even call it joy—is the passion of looking at and reacting to and assimilating the life of this earth. It derives from such commonplace things as breathing sea air, setting one foot in front of the other, feeling well, hearing birds sounding, getting into a car and starting it up to go somewhere, thinking back on the events of the day before and knowing that even though they were unremarkable I would love to live them over again. In Cronig's Market yesterday, everything about it, everything my eyes saw and my hands did, felt memorable and desirable and worth doing over again.

I am talking about a confident, elated involvement and interest in life (you can simplify it by calling it joie de vivre), which is not something consciously developed but which, genetically and experientially, is just there, as automatic as a little motor.

However, like all motors, this little motor, I have found, can switch off. One day as I am pushing a basket in Cronig's Market, all of a sudden shockingly, I realize that what I am looking at seems only to be painted there and that I am having no feeling about any of it. I am a robot pushing a basket with no alive connection to basket, or hands on metal, or other people pushing baskets, or shelves of groceries and mounds of fruits and vegetables. I see a bin of perfect-looking reddened peaches. I pick one up to test it for ripeness. In my mind is a response to my action's being successful—the peach is soft—but no sensation whatsoever about the pleasurable act of testing a peach.

I select four of the peaches automatically, put them in my basket along with the carton of skim milk, the jar of low-fat mayonnaise, the can of low-sodium organic vegetable soup. But there is no connection between me and these things in that basket. There they are, static and with no sound track. And here am I, with the wires gone soundless that usually connect me to groceries in a basket.

I stand there realizing that my little motor has switched off. Helplessly, I look at peaches that are not peaches as I know them, realizing that, inexplicably, my lively connection to peaches, to the world, and my interest in it, has gone. Worse yet, I know from experience that it can stay gone, for days, or even, I'm afraid, for weeks, for this is not a new phenomenon. It has happened to me before. I also know that "if it gets bad enough, the experts call it depression."[5] Neuterness sets in and then perplexity and then, of course, fear (not necessarily in that order). All things negative can settle in and stay. Until one day, unexpectedly, the little motor starts up again, and happiness is back.

Everyone knows that happiness comes and goes, depending on many things. And I imagine that happiness in old age can't coexist with serious troubles caused by aging. I imagine it can't abide, either, with the grief or the empathy one feels for the grave illnesses of family or friends or for all those deaths that occur with such saddening frequency. That is a kind of suffering in which I would not hope or even expect to feel any sort of happiness at all. At the memorial service last fall for my longtime and wonderful friend Agnes, I was involved solely in the grief I felt for the suffering she had had to endure before she died, and with my rebelliousness at the loss of her. Or so I thought.

And yet, coming out of the church into a gold and crisp October afternoon, I knew subconsciously that the little motor, though for the moment barely sounding, was still going underneath the heaviness of my sorrow. I knew, because I could see and feel the blue of the sky and the incandescent yellow of the maples in the church yard. I was having the feeling of life even in the experience of grief. I knew life to be there—saw it and felt it. And I had confidence that it was there. I had the conviction of a presence of feeling, quite different from the absence of feeling, which is depression.

And then, as I walked down the road to my car and opened the door to climb into it, I had the sudden, unwelcome thought that I had not been solely involved in my grief for Agnes back there in the church; I had not been, and was not now, exclusively involved with thoughts of Agnes. Oh, not at all. I remembered, and admitted guiltily, that as I sat there in the pew with my head bowed, my concern about Agnes had begun to be interwoven with sneaking, fearful concerns about myself, about my own possible illness, and of course, about my sometime, certain death. Commencing to weave in and out of my memories of Agnes's wasted face, along with the sound of the minister's purportedly reassuring words, "The Lord giveth and the Lord taketh away," were visions of myself all cremated into a dreadful powder, and the people sitting there in that church mourning *me*, who also had had a face wasted from cancer, and who had finally, after months of the cat-and-mouse game of that disease, died of it.

And now the sky did not appear a thrilling blue, and the yellow of the leaves were no more than just another maple tree turning yellow in the autumn.

I have thought about this for days, and I have come to the conclusion, which is, I must say, unsettling and challenging, that the most intimate and seriously troubling loss of happiness comes not wholly from clean concerns about the declining lives of others—their loneliness, their futility, their illnesses, their deaths—but partly, perhaps even basically, from the significance these casualties have for my own life and limb, all of which I view as blueprints for my own displacement, collapse, and demise. Happiness is lost, in other words, not only through concern about what is happening or can happen or has happened to others but, more lastingly, through fear of what could happen similarly to me.

If this is, in moderation, an excusable human feeling, and I imagine it is, I ought to feel less shocked by my discovery of it. "You're only human" can be a comforting phrase, and possibly I should be wise enough to admit it. Yet, as an expression of real and underlying fear, my associative and mixed concerns about Agnes can't be dismissed as being "only human." No. I wish for a cleaner involvement with my true friend Agnes. I wish to get rid of the distracting fear that what has happened to Agnes can happen to me, which separates me from her, which minimizes her death as it maximizes fear of mine. I see the proportions of that fear, I see how it can distort, how it can tamper with the abundance of loving.

And so I see that besides my legitimate suffering caused by the tragedies of others, there is another kind of suffering altogether, an illegitimate suffering based not on real, living tragedies but on fanciful, imagined ones, a suffering I bring upon myself through the vexation of spirit that is called, among other things, worry. The self-centered thoughts that took me away from Agnes were, to put it another way, worry.

"Worry" is a good, everyday word to stick with, and somehow to me a more natural one than its overworked counterpart, "anxiety." Dangerously, even, it is the harmless-feeling word that people toss off about themselves without thinking about it, or without any deep sense of its implications. But scratch a worrier and you will find fear—which is, of course, the guts of worry.

Because I know worry to its core, and dread it, I have created for myself a workable image of the word. It forms a latticed black iron gate with a sign on it—Keep Out—standing across a path and preventing a spirited thing—the personification of happiness—from continuing its frank-hearted course. Frowning worry impeding smiling happiness.

But is it selfish to want happiness? When all around me people I know, some of whom I love, are suffering and dying, is it monumentally and in a bad way self-absorbed to want to be happy in the face of their suffering?

And is it a moral irresponsibility to talk of the joy of living in a world drenched in misery? Am I selfishly detached from suffering in the world—South Africa, Bosnia, inner cities, the homeless? Should I be "involved in mankind" so that "every man's death diminishes me?"[6]

And is it selfish to be relieved that my little joy motor is ticking away, even after my friend Agnes's memorial service?

But sense and sensibility tell me that no, it is not wrong to want to enjoy being alive, even though it is my friend who is dead, not me; even though millions all over the world are suffering. Reason tells me that I am not depriving them of my concern by allowing myself to enjoy being alive, and that my intense response to and involvement in living is simply my way of praising and affirming living. I reassure myself that insistence on one's own happiness is as natural and as strong as sunshine and is in all people.

But specifically, what about my own day-to-day happiness, which seems to relate so profoundly to my husband? Am I a less than loving wife if I yell at the top of my lungs with the joy of diving into cold surf on a summer morning while my husband sits at home in his study, alone and stoic?

At lease thirty times a day, passing Nick's study as I walk down the long, narrow hall from the front vestibule to the kitchen, I look in, or I speak in passing, or I don't; but always in some way I am grabbed, even stricken, by the sight of Nick just sitting there in the same spot, in the same chair, in deep quietness and in solitude.

This is because I love him. And it is because of my compassion for him. But it is also, I know, to a certain extent, because I feel guilt over not being in that same sad situation, and because "my stronger guilt defeats my strong intent."[7]

All day long I walk up and down that long hall on the woven Iraqi rug of reds and purples and oranges, from early in the morning with a brisk step, till after dinner in the evening with a slow step, for I am always heading somewhere—to the kitchen (and from there out to my tent), or back from that part of the house to my own room, or to the front door to go somewhere. There is always a plan in my movements and an energy, except after dinner on my way to bed. And nine-tenths of the time as I pass Nick's room, there are his crossed knees—all that can be seen of him through the half-open door—and on them his hands spread out empty, or with a magazine in them; and the radio's classical music always on, turned low. But musical sound never seems to alter the silence of the unmoving crossed knees, of the deep, drawn-out quiet in the room, in the man.

I am like a train traveling back and forth from destination to destination, past a station once used and now empty, as I walk up and down that long, narrow hall that is the shape of a train track.

This morning, passing Nick's room on my way out to my tent, I heard the low perpetualness of strings that is Vivaldi, telling of life going quietly on as usual in there. I turned as always to look at the crossed knees, the quiet hands.

Then I stopped, deciding spontaneously to do the unusual and to go in to him and sit down on the couch for a while.

"Hi ho," I said jocularly, unnaturally, I suppose to make light of the unexpectedness of this action or to make it seem the casual, usual thing, which of course it was not.

Nick doesn't fall in with artifice, and so he said nothing. But he swiveled his chair around to face me, and regarded me with quiet eyes. Silence. But I'm used to that. If you expect the formality of a response from Nick, forget it. He replies only if there is something he wants to say.

"I guess I'll use up those artichokes for lunch," I said. "Shall I?"

"There's not much *to* them. But if you want."

"I guess I might as well. They've been there for days."

We sat in silence. I had come in with the idea of talking but was finding nothing to say. I turned idly and looked through the glass doors to the field that slopes down to the pond. "There's the little family," I cried.

"They're there all the time now. They're always there."

"I count three goslings. How many are there, do you know?"

"Four."

"I think that's the most splendid sight. The grandeur of those two geese—they call them 'sentinel'—male and female equally protecting, the vigilance, the dignity of those two. Would that most human babies got that kind of absolute attention."

Silence.

In a minute, Nick swiveled his chair a few inches, back toward its usual position, and reached to pick up a magazine lying on the table. "There's an article in this *Economist* you should read. About Perot. Wait'll you read it."

"Terrible?"

"Well, you won't like him."

"I must read it. Remind me."

He put the magazine back on the table. Sat back in his chair.

Again there was silence.

"I have the Alexander Technique group this afternoon," I said. "At Miriam's. If Rebecca should call while I'm out in my tent, would you take the message please, darling?"

"Yes."

"Well." I sat on for a few more minutes—token minutes, you might say. Then I got up. "Well, I'll be on my way to my tent."

He smiled up at me. "You do that," he urged strongly, but kindly. And, with relief?

But I didn't walk out of there with relief. No. I did not. I left the room in a hesitant, uncommitted way, even a defeated way.

I am in my tent, preparing to sum up some of the insights that have surfaced during the past weeks. I am looking out at the tall grass of the field that, in its response to the variability of the wind, has an obedience that is no less beautiful than a human dance, or maybe even more so. At one moment the grasses' stillness is shaken into a sudden supple whipping from side to side. Then there is a shivering lessening of movement; at the same time, beyond the almost motionless front wall of grass around my tent, a section of skirmish can be seen, a slight, momentary thrashing. Then out there, too, comes a sobering, a cessation, and finally the loveliest languid slow bending from side to side.

A sign to me to pay attention to what I am here to do, and to try to figure out whether my happiness has to be dependent on Nick's happiness. Or if it doesn't, what is the meaning of such unilateral joy? Is it good? Or is it, as it feels to me, bad?

I am torn between feeling that it is bad and thinking that it is not bad. Though, realizing that untethered joy has been possible for me even when Nick was in a time of solitary and detached melancholy, I have to admit that, on rare occasions of being momentarily freed of the obligation for responsibility and caretaker concerns and acute dependency on the ups and downs of Nick's well-being, a sudden, fountainlike surge of happiness has risen in me. I feel good while it happens but bad afterward.

So here is guilt, that archdestroyer. For suddenly it occurs to me that there is a strong element, in all this, of the old obligation to deprive myself of happiness simply because my brother and sister were deprived of it and, in a more immediate way—an old trickle-down pattern—to deprive myself of happiness now because my husband seems mostly without it.

And so I ask myself: Do I deserve happiness?

The answer, coming not from my head but from the ancestral texture of my being, is no. I have never believed that I deserved happiness, and childhood imprints being what they are, perhaps I never will.

But at the same time, even though I have an inbred conviction of being undeserving of happiness because of my brother's and sister's lack of it, and even though this ancient habit of guilt contaminates the compassion I have for my husband, it has never had any lasting effect on the delirious joy it is natural for me to feel.

Whereas fear! That is another thing. It pulls down the shades, it blots out the sun, it camouflages reality with the colors of fantasy, it blows apart my fragilely knitting integrity. And it does, with such a dreary, unnerving monotony, deny, deny, deny.

So I have to conclude that guilt can accuse happiness, can in a way punish happiness, but that it does not extinguish happiness in the crushing way that fear does.

I am struggling with the polarities of fear and happiness, and with guilt in the wings always waiting to make its entrances and its exits, its little raids of temporary destruction.

But if guilt is an unpleasant performance, fear is far worse than that. Fear destroys. And now, grown old, I am struggling with the ultimate prophecies it presents—the loss of health, vigor, looks, self-identity, people I love; in other words, the loss of everything, including, of course, life itself.

I am struggling mostly, though, with fear about the loss, inherent in the predictions of all those desolate impairments, of that marvelous little motor of joy that can hum away with such liveliness and verve and with such a revelation and bestowal of life—air, insects, railways, ponds, faces, eyes, fields of grass, old houses, new houses, dogs, deer, bedspreads, hands, fragrances, thunder, teacups, wine, sun, hard rain, wind, icicles, the color red, a blue truck, a pink sunset, stillness, the right word, lilacs.

I think it is safe to say that this joy of living is, both metaphorically and actually, the very breath of life to me and that without it, I am only part of what I can be. So the little motor's capriciousness, and the consequences of it, warn me that I need to find something besides an involuntary source of happiness, something that is not sensation-al but that is in a secure way *grasped* by me as being sensibly and reliably entrenched, something perhaps directed by reason—an inner bedrockness—that can assure the continuance of that precious source of happiness too frequently shut off.

I may even be talking about the unaccentuated marvelousness of normalcy. I may be talking, even, about peace of mind. Or, these days, I may be feeling that happiness is simply the absence of fear.

4 The Strawberry and the Tigers

A TIME of darkness. I will begin with the darkest part.

One afternoon last week, the four members of "The Music Group" met in our house for the first time this season, two of them summer people who have just returned to the island after a winter away.

They all trooped in, Claude, Thomas and Irma, carrying their instrument cases.

Embraces. Here we are, another winter has passed and we're all still alive, I thought but did not say. Thomas, eighty, had a brush with death in April and now wears a pacemaker. Claude, eighty-one, also had a brush with death in December—open-heart surgery to replace a faulty valve. Claude's wife, Hildegard, just weeks before this meeting, had a stroke, seriously affecting her speech. She is a seventy-nine-year-old scholar and teacher of comparative literature, a novelist and a poet, a woman whose distinguished career and life have been the "word."

And all this in my house, where my husband moves slowly and patiently as a result of those two small strokes; where an elderly man who does odd jobs has had an angina heart attack; where a sixty-year-old woman who cleans and cooks has spent a winter of chemotherapy and radiation to combat a return of breast cancer and has no medical insurance because her husband, who had the insurance for both of them, just recently lost the job that provided it.

That night I woke up and lay there thinking, worrying—worrying about those people, yes. But in addition, as at Agnes's funeral, worrying with vivid and deep concern about myself. Would this happen to me? What assurance did I have that it wouldn't?

Of course I had no assurance that none of those awful things would happen to me! In the dark, I felt my space crowding, crowding with hampered, stricken people, I felt more and more of them coming into it, surrounding me, pressing around me, filling the darkness with their mute and passive suffering. And there I stood, in the center of this silent congregation, the only one unscathed.

There was something delusive and shocking about this imagined sensation. I felt cornered in it. I thought of Sartre's *No Exit.* It was then I saw, I think, that indeed there was no exit for me. I saw a reality. I saw—and it was a preposterously hard admission for me—that though I was still unscathed, there was no way on this earth that I would remain so forever.

This thought was so impossible that I reared up in bed, turned on the lamp, and, frantic for rescue, reached for the little paperback of Zen I had on my night table. I had bought it only the week before on the recommendation of my next-door neighbor and had skimmed through it with interest. Wasn't there something in it about a strawberry? Something helpful about a strawberry?

Strawberry, strawberry . . . I found the page; in fact, on one side of it I had put a yellow sticker paper as a reminder to read it again.

"There is a centuries old Buddhist parable," I read, "about a man who was being chased by a tiger. In his flight from it he dove over the side of a cliff and clutched a vine hanging there. As the tiger paws away above him he looks below and sees another tiger at the base of the cliff. To make the situation irreversible, two mice have begun to gnaw the vine.

"At that moment, the man spots a luscious red strawberry and, holding onto the vine with one hand, he picks the strawberry and eats it. It is delicious!"[8]

I closed the book. The idea of a perfectly well person standing among unwell people and suffering at the prospect of becoming unwell appeared with utter clarity as absurd and unsound; so much so that for a moment I knew this entirely and safely and even complacently.

"You can't live that way." My doctor's admonition came into my head, rebukingly, as he had said it. "You must stop being the 'worried well,'" he said with the honest severity that makes me trust him.

A simple, plain warning. A tiger above me, a tiger below me, and me hanging by a fraying vine.

Of course. That's the way it is. Except that here is this strawberry.

And so, even though I know this is the last moment of my life, I won't waste it. I will eat this strawberry.

What was eventually to become for me an internalized formula for dealing with fear began with the reading of that parable about two tigers and a strawberry. It may have seemed at first glance to be a superficial, simplistic, and even gruesome Grimm's fairy tale, but in the long run, the image of a ripe, red strawberry, making plain the fact that "now" is the only sure place, became more and more profound, and turned out to be uncannily applicable to so much in so surprising a way.

5 Who I Am

IN THE beginning I talked about the beauty of wise old faces, enviously and with the knowledge that what they had I felt I did not have, but also with the conviction that what they had I would have to have if I were to live my old age in relative peace and happiness. I knew then, absolutely, that I couldn't hope to encompass the changes and fears of old age unless I made contact with some part of myself that was not perishable—like the spirit of those old people with wise and beautiful faces—something that would never be subject to change. Beauty, those old faces reminded me, is everlasting.

But in the searching I have only just begun, I see that I am a long, long way from finding a thorough answer to that very fundamental question of how to locate, and to extract from all the dross, whatever of enduring value there is in me.

And also, it is becoming increasingly apparent that I must find out whether there is anything entire and vital in me that has not, in some tenacious, even unalterable way, been defined by my relation to a man. What I mean is: What could I be, separate from my husband?

If there is something in me, underneath the wrinkled, anxious face I see in the mirror, that can soften it and give it spirit and light (not for the sake of the face but for the sake of the spirit), then let me try to find it. For behind the persona, the spirit struggles.

Yesterday I suddenly began to wonder what my face had looked like when I was a young girl. And then I remembered a picture of me that Father always kept on the chiffonier in his bedroom. I even remembered the frame it was in—gilded wood swinging between two posts on pedestals.

I went up right away to the attic. And in the trunk where I keep old photographs and family documents, I found it.

There I was ("Margaret, 14 years old," it said on the back) wearing the paisley dress with the boat neck piped in brown velvet that I remembered so well, designed by myself and made by Q. B. Jackson, Mother's inexpensive and resourceful dressmaker. Blond hair brought down along my face, which was oval like the frame, was caught back, then brought out to lie in ringlets over both shoulders. Across my forehead were feathers of bangs cut by myself and looking it, too.

"You've never learned how to do your hair, Peggoty." Father said this simply, not critically; no offense was taken, because no offense was intended. I had been thirty years old when Father had said this to me one morning at breakfast. (And he was right. I knew it. I was always fussing with my hair to try new ways, none of them ever quite right.) Thereafter I had applied myself to the project of finding the right way to do my hair, which eventually I found. "I like the new way you're doing your hair," Father said one day in his quiet way.

I studied the photograph raptly. I was *seeing* this girl. For the first time. The smiling mouth had lost no basic individuality in the self-consciousness of being photographed, though its discomfort was evident in a faint stiffness.

I was struck by the fact that one side of my face was noticeably different from the other side. I put a hand over first one side and then the other. Was it agreeable, candid, the left side, with a fuller, more open, hopeful, even playful look? Whereas was the right side more condensed, experienced? Was I imagining this?

But, yes, there was a deeper knowingness to the left eye, and a more open kindness. And was there feeling, and fun, over a base of—sadness?

Was the eye of the right side a bit narrower and vulnerable and, above all, really sad? Was it better than the other eye? More together, somehow? That eye knew everything, it did. It knew, and knew, and knew, and was wise.

Ho hum, a split personality? Split between sense and sensibility, yes?

A decency in the whole face suggested that this girl wouldn't want to let you down, and if she did, would suffer. Please trust me, she begged, longing to trust and be trusted, wanting decency in this world.

But it was the natural young dignity in the posture of head, neck, and shoulders that struck me above all else. It was the dignity, or call it freedom, of being able to be the way she essentially was, before she learned to become the way she essentially was not.

I tried to transfer this dignity to myself, to see if it would fit, so to speak. I tried to wear it, for a moment, to see whether it belonged on me. It did not, I thought. And anyway, back then, of course, I hadn't even known I had it, so how would I know what it felt like now?

But it's there, I thought, somewhere.

Me, at age fourteen

*   *   *

I realized that the more I studied this girl, the more I found in her. Was I putting things into this girl that weren't there?

Certainly, though, unmistakable was the promise of suffering in the whole face. It was open to everything. Shielded by nothing. But, as well, there was no resignation there. None. This girl would never give up.

This girl had character.

Why did you think I didn't have character, Mother?

"That girl's okay." My voice did not startle me, and I only felt in it the expulsion of a lifetime of doubt. I have become quite cruddy, I thought with shame and hope. I was a lot better then than now.

But what *am* I now?

To begin with, what do I certainly know about myself? What is obvious to me and to everyone else about Margaret Scott Howe Sloan Freydberg? And also, what do I certainly know about how it feels to be me, in my life situation?

I was born in the United States, of Scottish and British descent. The knowledge of my Scotch ancestry is something I use to define myself, for I like the thought of being Scotch and take pleasure in what I consider to be Scotch characteristics—passion, for one. (Even Scotch Puritanism is passionate.) In fact, come to think of it, an awareness of being Scotch is pridefully in my consciousness.

I am Presbyterian raised and indoctrinated (yes, that is the word for it), and the knowledge of this is always just

Our house on Stonewall Pond

below the surface and manifest, alas, in the contradictions of my puritan-rebel behavior. But like breathing sea air and knowing it is sea air I'm breathing, much of my conscious behavior is part and parcel of the awareness of that awful religious climate I was brought up in.

My geographical location is the island of Martha's Vineyard, Massachusetts, surrounded by the Atlantic Ocean; Rochester in upstate New York is my birthplace—my past but still innerly my present.

The material conditions of my life are this beautiful island; the sea; the fields around the house; the pond below it; the brook running beside it; the comfortable, agreeable house itself; its furnishings; its music; its books; its kitchen; its food; its sun-filled rooms. And seventy-five miles away, the fine old city of Boston.

I have a few close woman friends, every one of them fascinatingly different from the others, and they are one of the foundations of my life.

I have a few very minor talents—among them painting and piano playing—which characterize me, I suppose, as being artistically inclined.

I am a writer (a published one), and I know, in an always pervasive and grateful way, that writing comes, needfully, before any other use of myself.

I know what my looks are, constantly and consciously. I know all the implications of my face and figure.

I know what my body is, and I know how I make it unnecessarily suffer through my tensions and fears. Yet in spite of that, I am healthy.

I know that integrity exists in me and that even though it doesn't always work, it keeps on trying to.

I know my values and that I have an innocent passion for decency, a rage to *be* decent, to want others to be decent, to want the world to *be* decent. So I know myself to be, innately, a decent person.

I am aware of my emotions, which are intense; I am aware of my sensitivity, which is intense; I generally catch my weaknesses, intense too. I sense my innocence, or childlikeness. I am in daily contact with my insecurities—either angers or prejudices or judgments. I perceive my pretensions. I wince at the constancy of my guilt. I am beginning to recognize and to understand my egoism's origins and performances. And above all, I live with my fears and see the extent to which Panicky Peggy, from the word go, has grown in me like a thick and spreading fungus, has *become* me, has become perhaps the most controlling part of me. I have learned, regrettably, that I aim to please, with all the crap that that entails. I thoroughly know the way the tragedy of my family circumstances, and my upbringing, has affected me. I know both the profundities and the complexities of my marriage.

I possess a strong life force, or a force for wanting positivism, for going ahead, for not wanting to be downed. No matter what adversities there have been in my life, I have always, after being toppled, righted myself. It is as though I have a base in me, like those pear-shaped papier-mâché Russian dolls weighted in the bottom which, when struck, wave and wobble madly to and fro, but then gradually wave and wobble more slowly and finally grow still.

I am always aware of the incomparable experience of having a family I love.

I have two children—a daughter, Laidily, and a son, Sam.

Nick and I call them "our" children, though they are mine through my marriage to Sam Sloan. But Nick has been their father since Laidily was eighteen and Sam thirteen, two years after Sam, Sr., died.

There was a lot of adaptation, naturally, for everyone, and for many years. But as they grew, we all grew. And the end result was that Nick loved my children and grandchildren as much as, or more than, he ever loved anyone; and they loved him.

Our ties are vital and deep and with an ongoing electric interest. Sam's two daughters, Tamara and Emily, visit us a lot and have profound ties to Nick and me. They seek Nick as seer and rely on his wisdom—a guidance they seek from him, not one he thrusts on them.

I see myself in my daughter and son, and I see them in me. Unfortunately, though, I have an uncertain sense of myself as a mother, because I was young and unknowing when I had my children, and some of the troubles they have had in their lives are a result of this, I know. So when I think of myself as a mother, I often uneasily feel that I am not worthy of being one. The sentiments on Mother's Day cards don't seem to describe me at all.

But although I often anguish over the kind of young mother I was, I have finally grown to know how much my children and grandchildren are fulfilling a part of my self-identity.

All that, in a more or less superficial way, is the picture of myself.

Now I must try to see what, in that autobiographical definition of a woman's life, seems essential insofar as the happiness of old age is concerned, and what is not. What can be lost, such as fading and worn appearances? And what can remain, something that I firmly and religiously know is under my skin?

* * *

What can be lost:

My looks.

Material conditions: Land, house, possessions, through financial changes and/or through lack of emotional stamina to keep things up.

People: Friends, acquaintances, community relationships, which, heaven knows, are so often subject to change in old age.

Minor talents and accomplishments: Through the loss of energy and capacity—like playing the piano.

Writing: If I "lose it," as they say, because of physical or mental deterioration.

As I write this, I caution myself that I must not let my guesses about the possible losses of the future incline me toward dwelling lugubriously on them. Because if I fall into that old habit, I will be violating my new and ardent belief in the enjoyment of a strawberry while waiting to be devoured by a tiger. I see that what can be misused about my knowledge of all these possible losses is that, way before I have to, I could center my self-definition on imagining myself as a woman who has been exiled forever from the country that was native to her. Moment by moment I might be finishing myself off in my imagination before—perhaps even long before—I actually will be finished off. I could even, through a concept and through the awful power of worry, make myself into something that in fact, at this present moment, I am not.

And so instead, what I am hoping to do here, dispassionately, is only to admit and to accept the possibility of what can in the future be perishable, for the purpose of looking at what can be imperishable. I am hoping simply to find what there is in me that can endure rewardingly, hoping to find my own immortality within the confines of my mortality.

*   *   *

Now I must try to see beyond what I think could be lost, to what I think could remain.

My life force: Debatable. I'm afraid I will have to put this most valuable resource of mine in a category all by itself. For I wonder whether, if I have a seriously demoralizing illness or if I become senile, I will at last be totally without that deep and seemingly renewable well of positivism that has been the blessing of my life. I assume that such a force takes energy; that the passion for being alive and the determination to stay upright must be dependent on some kind of energy, either psychic or physical or both, which illness or senility could diminish or else do away with entirely. I would like to be able to count on the continuance of my life force, but I do not know whether I can.

My integrity: Such as it is, which to the last gasp I hope can help me find artless and mindful ways to live.

My heart: Which until it stops, can love, even though its first purpose would be gone if Nick were gone.

My love of nature: Let me always be where I can see leaves and grass and the sea.

My values: Which are unalterable.

My inmost being: Do I mean the "thinking" me, the mind that per unspoken agreement with me and all males has been labeled lightweight and that I have kept buried, inactive, hushed-up, the core of myself that is independent of any other person, that gives expression to itself and to others through definition of itself, not through a relationship to a man?

Yes. I know, I absolutely know, that the most persistently indistinguishable element of my being—that aliveness down there in the dark that for my whole life has ticked away like a strong heart—has been my longing to have a life *not* defined by a relationship to a man, a longing for the independence of my uncoerced self, a self that has survived as powerfully as my need to measure it unequally and unfavorably with a husband.

In short, I see the most dynamic parts of me—a necessity for my self, and a necessity for a man—as the two greatest and most opposingly powerful factors of my life.

As I review what I have put down, it is clear that those things which can be subject to change—looks, material conditions, talents, social satisfactions—do not appear to be substantial bases for the pursuit of happiness in old age, since they are more than likely to go.

But those qualities that could survive and are not predictably subject to change, could be it seems to me, reliable bases for essential living. Indispensable to the pursuit of happiness and to happiness itself, those are the qualities, I believe, from which courage could come.

At lunch one day, Nick and I were talking about self-identity and my interest in Erik Erikson's definition of it. Suddenly I asked him, "What do you think of as your self-identity?"

He thought a long time, typically. Then he spoke his thoughts, with long pauses between short sentences.

"I think I'm fairly decent. It's important to me. If I weren't decent, it would be painful to me.

"I suppose I'm generous.

"I have a temper, but I get over it.

"I like comfort.

"My looks are okay, I guess. I don't dislike my looks, but they're all right. I know I'm not handsome.

"I don't worry about my health. Right now, of course"—he had an intestinal ailment—"but I'm not a hypochondriac."

That's all. And insofar as that is all, that is Nick. I'll do him the honor of making no comment—his way.

My marriage to Nick has been an all-encompassing, almost total definition of my existence, and since I am now beginning a search for an understanding of how I define myself, I should begin it by acknowledging how immensely I am defined by my relation to one man, and the extent to which this attachment figures in the way I live my life, and the way I am.

The more I think about what goes on in me about Nick, and what goes on between us, the more it is apparent that the focal purpose of my life with him has been to use myself for him and that my living has been controlled in large part for forty-seven years by this inescapable need. Although it must be clear by now that the losing of myself in a man is not new and began with my father. For the first nineteen years of my life I was linked, as though umbilically, to him. Then for the next nineteen years, I allowed myself to be, even asked to be, absorbed by my husband Sam. And after Sam died, in the forty-seven years of my marriage to Nick, this need has continued to be a large part of how I feel and see myself.

Our marriage has been, on and off, along with all the beneficence and basic harmony, a combative one. Like most marriages, it has been composed of pluses and minuses. But in an overall and basic way, ours has been mostly pluses, possibly because I truly, enormously love Nick. And so it is habitual for me often to wonder about what has held us together for all these years. But when I am in the throes of questioning what the solid base of my marriage is, I tend to forget that that solid base is a true love for the essence of the man. And I believe (though I can never be certain, since he hasn't said it in so many words) that he is held to me by the same kind of love. Anyway, inseparable we are, inseparable we have always been. For better or for worse.

We are inseparable for many reasons:

Because of a basic and imperishably mutual attraction.

Because of what, inadvertently, we give each other of ourselves that works toward our betterment. For example, in living with Nick's steadfastness and truth, there has come to be, in me, a subliminal and often conscious reflection of that gentle man that is always in our house, like flowers blooming.

Because of the intertextural sharing of two lives. "Oh look, there are the goslings!"

And paradoxically, we are inseparable because of combat (although there is none left now). But for most of our lives together, up until five years or so ago, we fought, sporadically but intensely. We hurt each other. I think we have both always been fighting for autonomy, which apparently we were constantly trying to deny each other. Yet I feel there has been an aliveness to our battles, a sort of vitality, and that they have been a signal to us that our basic rivalries should be brought to the surface and heeded and dealt with. I think that our combat has been essential to our progress. I know it has. It has been a lively and necessary engagement. Because of it, we have never let anything be swept under the rug.

And again, paradoxically, we are inseparable because of my mindless, indoctrinated obligation to be responsible for a loved person, which is so much a part of my self-identity—the image given me in my childhood of the ministering female I should be. I grew up badly needing to protect and, badly, this deep-seated, anciently habitual act, which Nick both wants and does not want, goes on and on.

I am not forgetting that woman is instinctually mothering and that my instinct and my good fortune (up to a point) have been to want to look after the man I love. And I know that this is good for him and for me (again, up to a point). But I also know, increasingly with Nick's increasing fragility, that I am being drawn irresistibly back into the historic excesses of nurselike attentiveness to my afflicted brother and sister, which I not only absorbed but was instructed in, in my childhood and forever after, and which—even though a part of Nick still wants it—I know he has come to dread and to fear. I do try constantly to stop the supervising and the worry, and I congratulate myself that I never stoop quite so low as to remind Nick to take his pills. Sometimes, though, as I grieve and lose sleep about his solitude and his sadness and his fragility, the image of *La Pietà* is superimposed upon myself, and for a moment I am it and, in a delicious and comfortingly terrible way, love being it.

And lastly, we are inseparable because of my need to be protected, which, in innate and chivalrous maleness, Nick is responsive to. For oh how I long for male protection, male support—a rock to lean on. And Nick is that. I am told that no woman ever completely loses a buried (or not so buried) longing for the comforting arms of her father, both metaphorical and actual. I am sure I never will. But I certainly would like to diminish the funny, awful power of my dependence on this from Nick.

* * *

I know that what Nick intrinsically is does not connect with what I intrinsically am, that my inmost being is unknown to him. One reason, perhaps, is that for so long my inmost being has been unknown even to me. And so I do think that no matter how much we both grow and know, we will always be, at bottom, unknowable to each other.

Even so, Nick has given me the self-identity of a woman who loves her husband and is loved by him. And though, perhaps unreasonably, I have wanted more from both of us, that, with all my heart, is what I want the most.

Two rabbits on the evening lawn. And a robin. In the quiet of the pond—no wind now, and the sound of sea surf remote and distant—the robin keeps up his lilting music, over and over again, unable to stop.

We eat our dinner and drink our wine, saying to each other that the swordfish needs lemon, that you can salt it endlessly and not improve its taste but that a squeeze of lemon does it; saying that we are tired and should go to bed as soon as the dishes are done, arguing a little about which of us is less tired and should therefore do the dishes.

We wash the dishes, of course, together.

Nick and I and the robin's song and the rabbits on the evening lawn, and the pond cooling and darkening. He and I together, rabbit by rabbit, robin by robin, have built this structure, this gentle, tireless habit. Here is an evening harmony, the contest of the day past, all passion spent, a unison not built by words or minds.

I fold a damp towel and hang it on the towel rack. And as I am doing this, Nick comes up behind me and slides his arms around my waist. This puts great ease into me. I stand quietly against him, resting my hands over his.

Nick and me

6 Seeing the World through Self-Located Eyes

MID-SUMMER (like middle age giving one the complacent confidence that it will go on forever and with much more blooming still to come) was now substantially—permanently, it seemed—entrenched.

Black-eyed Susans replaced daisies in the field around the tent, and heavy-scented privet pushed at the rose-fragrant air, for these were the weeks when everywhere dense masses of wild roses spilled over old stone walls and split-rail fences.

Yet even with the distraction of my senses' delirium over this profligate perfumery and color, I was always thinking about what a more thorough, a more entire attentiveness might be, a more intellectual attentiveness, you might say. Couldn't attentiveness go beyond sensation? Shouldn't it? Wasn't it essential to try to sharpen attentiveness, which had to do, didn't it, with living in the moment of the strawberry?

And then July was suddenly, alarmingly, August. Instead of so much birdsong, there were crickets in the long silences. And instead of black-eyed Susans in the field around my tent, there was the depth of goldenrod like the color of sun. In the evening, I needed a sweater, sitting out on the deck with Nick.

Autumn came, with its great orchestral finale.

And finally, one day, I had to dismantle the tent, for it had become too cold to work in it, even with my sweater sleeves pulled down over my wrists and a blanket over my knees.

Back in the house I shifted over without too much disorientation to working in a habitation rather than in a close-to-nature shelter, while watching through my window the branches of the trees grow bare and then the first snowflakes of November begin to sift down.

Winter was here, undeniable, unwelcome winter, the season for which a stoic attitude has to be sought and adopted, the season for which I have always had to brace myself. Shortened daylight, interminable hours of darkness. Snow; its silencing, its covering of fields and beaches and roads and trees and frozen ponds, and of my spirit.

But attentiveness? I kept remembering the story of the tigers and the strawberry and that wonderful little seed of an idea that it planted in me. I kept remembering the fallacy of scenarios of the worst. And I kept telling myself that now is the only sure moment and that the way to be free of fear is to live in that moment.

One day I realized all at once that I was still unclear about the connection between attentiveness and being in the present moment. Strange, how hard it was for me to get this. But finally, yes, there it was, so simple as to be obvious: Attentiveness and being in the present moment are inseparable. You can't have one without the other. For attentiveness in its pure sense is to be objectively and undistractedly mindful about things as they truly are, without added subjective judgments. I cannot be truly mindful about the nature of this present moment unless I am paying unpreoccupied, nonjudgmental, exclusive attention to it. (Maybe this has been clear to others, but I haven't really clarified it for myself until now.)

Yet in spite of this knowledge, which remained stalematedly only that, I had to keep coaxing myself to pay attention. But it appears I simply did not know how. Without the colors and sounds and smells of summer, my so-called attentiveness seemed to be growing as dormant as the bare fields and leafless trees. Live in the moment, I scolded myself. Attention. Attention. Have a strawberry.

One winter afternoon I was struck down for a moment by an appalling feeling: Why does the finally accepted knowledge that I am not always going to be on this beautiful earth change everything so totally?

I was standing by a window looking out at the snow-covered fields around our house. I stood there and looked out the window at the crows gliding, hearing their sore-throated, rusty squawks, viewing them with melancholy and without any feeling, and with the unfamiliar reaction of not relating to them at all, of not putting myself into them, of the uselessness of putting myself into them.

A fearful quiet took me. There was something so empty about looking at this winter scene and thinking that it had no use, that its existence and its beauty didn't matter because soon, too soon, *I* would not be here to see it.

As well as being stilled, I was puzzled. I have the same eyes that looked at this yesterday and allowed me to see it alive-ly. I have the same capacity for aliveness that soared yesterday from the interest and the wonder of this scene.

Then what has changed today in the way I look at the world, as a result of the newly learned and accepted fact that I am old, and am not going to be here forever to see crows gliding over snow-covered fields? Why shouldn't I feel joy today as I did yesterday? Tell me. I am old, it is true, but I feel fine. I am not sick. I feel sprightly and energetic. My husband, whom I love, is in good health in spite of his two slight strokes. I live in a beautiful spot by the sea. Life interests me. I am not poor. I have work that I love and live by.

Am I without joy because winter is a kind of death, the opposite of bursting, flowering life, and so is a symbol of what I fear?

Whatever it is, I do not feel joy today. Indeed, I feel blank, I feel astonishingly neuter as I look out the window at the black busy crows and the long white fields. I feel the way I did when the wires connecting me to peaches in Cronig's Market went soundless.

Why is it necessary, in order to enjoy my existence, to believe that I must exist forever? Can it be possible to relate to what I am looking at only if I feel confident of endless longevity? Does my joie de vivre depend on the sense that my life will never come to an end?

I was struck right away by the nonsense of this. For one thing, if I'm not here to do the looking—I mean, if I am dead—what's this all about? And also, the co-relation I feel between me and the snow-covered fields and the crows I am looking at is not a co-relation at all, it is not mutuality. I am not connected to anything in the landscape but my seeing it, nor is it putting anything into me but its being there.

Nevertheless, I seem to be dependent on claiming it, on somehow using it. I seem to be dependent on a sense of my own immortality in order to savor and to love what I see; and to feel that unless an immortal self is observing the crows and the fields, there is not beauty there for me. Alan Watts says, "When each moment becomes an expectation, life is deprived of fulfillment, and death is dreaded for it seems that here expectations must come to an end."[9]

So what do I do about this senseless, disserviceable, yet powerfully controlling attitude? I asked myself as I turned away from the window.

Begin with one foot at a time, I advised myself. Start with a thorough recognition of this extraordinary aberration. Realize that it is an aberration. Realize, actually, that it is fear of the tigers waiting. Then try to turn off that fear, which in this case is adding something to the scene that is simply not there at this moment. In fact, come to think of it, since the tigers eventually have to do what they are there to do, shouldn't I try to find a way of not being continually downed by reminders of them? Isn't the danger in always remembering the two tigers, that I am living in a climate of constant presentiment, living in the fantasy of the future rather than in the reality of now? In other words, I wonder whether, in accepting the tigers, I am simply ratifying the prospect of a gruesome fate, living always in the gloom of that concept. Must I always look the tiger in the mouth?

No. Surely that is not the idea behind the parable.

But forget the tigers for a moment and try to concentrate on me *looking*, rather than only on *me*. Try to understand that everything about this way of looking at the crows and the fields is extraneous except the looking itself and is meaningless to me because of the overlay of me on it—the overlay of fearful me on it. I hadn't felt what I was looking at because of the shadow on it of my panic at the thought of not always being here to see it. Or possibly I was feeling the unimaginableness of a world without this throbbing viewer, me, in it. (I must start taking self-concern seriously.)

That approach seemed to suggest that I would have to see the world not habitually as I felt about it, but as it was, by itself, without putting myself into it. Which is to say that it is my way to view the circumstances of this world primarily in terms of how they make me feel. Yes. I am always editorializing, never a moment of not assessing or describing or sensationalizing what I'm in the act of doing.

Of course, I have an expressive nature, and I am a writer. And I am naturally joyous. I have always needed to take in the world and churn it up in there and then breathe it out in a great gasp of expressiveness. And I'm not denigrating the process, though it sounds that way, for it is an essential one for me, and lively. As Marianne Moore says, "One writes because one has a burning desire to objectify what it is indispensable to one's happiness to express."[10]

Nevertheless, I saw that the time had come to try to latch on to something besides the way life makes me *feel.*

One day, I had a momentary, sharp sense of how remarkable it would be to have a way of viewing crows and snow-covered fields without such needy, such self-located eyes. Wouldn't it be a new and unusually interesting experience, I thought with excitement, to look at a world that is not filtered by me, that loses me in the looking?

It was then, surprisingly, that I remembered I had once done just that, years and years ago, I think sometime in the seventies. It fascinates me, and encourages me, to realize that even way back then the process of my awakening had begun, that everything inner and outer that for so many years had been working for my growth had, for a few minutes on the shore of the sea one summer day twenty years ago, coalesced into a miraculous clarity.

This is what happened, as I wrote it afterward:

> A spent wave rushed up to where Nick and I were sitting, scalloping almost to our feet, then fizzing away and leaving the sand silver wet.
>
> I looked at the sand.
>
> I *saw* the sand.
>
> I saw that the sand had been left silver by the receding wave.
>
> Then, with a calm astonishment, I looked at the sea that had made the sand silver.
>
> Although the approach to it is complex, the experiencing of the fact of something as distinct from one's emotion about it is not in the least so. It is a simple, straightforward, marvelously easy miracle. This is what happened to me now. For the first time in my life, I saw the world outside of myself. The calf, too, pushing headfirst out of the birth canal, opens one great eye and sees the world for the first time. I saw space, saw it and knew it to be the other part of life—billions of people all over the world, busy, doing things. The world swarmed with people. Continents were dense with humanity—city streets, towns, villages, plains, prairies, deserts, tundras, mountains, all were black with the packed populations of the globe—like a round, ripe fruit black with ants. I was staggered to realize how many people there were in the world besides me and Nick, billions of them.
>
> The sense of division, of myself here and the world off there, of two entities existing but divided, grew overwhelming. Here I am, I marveled, but there is the world,

too. And as if further to reveal the world unknown to me, a distant plane droned across the immense, the endless sky.

I looked at the sea. And in looking at it, all at once I saw the fact of it, the life within it, and the rock I was sitting on, a part of it. I saw warm living shore, cold living sea, and for the moment, detached from my own involvement in earth and sea, I had an illumination of the oneness and the counterpoint of life. And in seeing this I had such a strong sense of *life*—not a feeling about it but an attentive comprehending of it—that I was taken out of myself in a calm, sensible way. Life is, I thought, with a sober thrill. It is not as I *see* it, but as it *is*.

I knew I had never felt this way—so huge and yet so simple, even empty. I was a hugeness of emptiness. I wanted there to be a continuance of silence between Nick and me, even a silence that would not end.

But. Almost immediately, no! I flung myself around to face Nick. "Listen," I cried, "life *is*! Do you know what I mean when I say that? Life *is*? I've just had the most magical moment. It's unbelievable. God, I hope I'm able to describe it to you. What it was, I suddenly saw that the sand was silver and that the sea had made it so, and then I looked at the sea and, there it was, the sea. There it was. And here I was. And I said to myself, 'Life *is*.' But oh heavens, how to describe it. *I* had nothing to do with it. I mean, it was there and I am here. Oh, this isn't saying it," I cried. "Oh damn, damn," I muttered, for like the receding wave, the feeling was already slipping away. I was aware still of emptiness, but it was an uneasy emptiness, with no color, no throb, no exultation, nothing of myself in it.

Life *is* . . . Well, those had been the words. And there they were. Except that now I wasn't feeling them, only thinking them. Their impact, what they had been significantly about, was not in me at all. Their capacity to lead somewhere had bled out of them, so that they were words that were no use as something to stir me, to generate a whole new feeling in me.

For a second I had a bewildering sense of loss, as though I had abandoned myself.

And so I thought: You can't say "life *is*," you have to say, "life is as *I* experience it." I cannot separate myself from life. No one can. I see it through my own eyes, and it is there to be taken into me and felt and used for *my* joy and *my* sorrow. Total objectivity is impossible, and the person who believes it of himself deceives himself.

A gull went floating, circling overhead, its cries lost in the sound of the surf. I had the sense of having given up something by deciding to talk about myself to Nick. The gull's cries told me this. I felt concentrated and befuddled and locked up within a darkness in myself. I looked up at the gull, at its casual soaring, and wished passionately for that. I wanted to release Nick. I felt I had him trapped. There was no such thing as the contented calm of the two of us together on the beach on a summer afternoon. No such thing at all.

A week or so after reading the scene of me and Nick and the sea, and thinking that perhaps it had returned to me after twenty years because I was at last ready to take it seriously, I was sitting one morning in my writing chair with a pencil in my hand and a yellow pad on my knees. Outside it was foggy and mild—one of those sudden unseasonable winter days. Fog is depressing to me, I thought. My spirits are gray, just like this day. Life can be gray, and sad, just like this day. I am growing old and this fog is symptomatic of the grayness, the low-key neuterness of my aging spirit.

And then suddenly, like seeing the sea and me as separate, I saw the fog and me as separate. And I said to myself: The fog's impact is surely different on me than on Nick, who *likes* fog and who is sitting in his study down the hall, seeing it too. Which means—doesn't it?—that the weather beyond our windows is not a verity in terms of its relation to me or to him, it is only a verity in and of itself. The reality of the fog is only in itself, not in the emotions it produces in my husband or me.

This was a cleansing and relieving moment. For I saw that the only exactitude for me in this particular moment was the existence of a self free of thoughts irrelevant to the reality of that moment (free, indeed, of thoughts, and so free to pluck the strawberry) plus the existence, outside, of the fog. Two separate exactitudes, two independences.

And then I wondered whether the more I could metaphorically defog myself in moments dense with dissatisfactions that were irrelevant to the exactitude of them, the more I could defog myself in greater and more threatening irrelevancies?

And such growing clarity could, couldn't it, eventually allow me to comprehend the paper-tiger sufferings for what they were and the strawberry for what it was?

But what if—and here is a thought to take me away from the prospect of the Elysian fields I seem to have promised myself that being in the present moment will be—the reality of now is no strawberry? What if I come to a place between a cliff and an abyss and am hanging by a fraying vine on which there is no strawberry, on which there is nothing? In other words, what if the reality of now becomes real suffering, not the kind for fools?

Zen has an answer, the only bearable one, I think. About real suffering, Zen teaches us to *be* the suffering, not to *bemoan* the suffering. If this here and now suddenly becomes not a fantasy of suffering but real suffering itself, one must *be* it, *feel* it, *act* it, but not *think* about it.

Alan Watts says that "pain is the nature of this present moment, and I can only live in this moment."[11]

And so I see that if I am in the grip of a serious emotional or physical problem, the most bearable way to handle it is to see and to accept the verity, the exactitude of that problem. For my salvation and peace of mind, I have to experience pain or fear as separate from my thoughts of it. In other words, in not compounding or confusing my essential suffering with all kinds of fears and conjectures of what may happen to me as a result of it, I am *being* the suffering—the kind that is not for fools. I *am* pain. I am not *thinking* pain.

"It seems that if I *am* afraid," Watts continues, "then I am 'stuck' with fear. But in fact I am chained to the fear only so long as I am trying to get away from it. On the other hand, when I do not try to get away I discover that there is nothing 'stuck' or fixed about the reality of this moment. When I am aware of this feeling without naming it, without calling it 'fear,' 'bad,' 'negative,' etc., it changes instantly into something else, and life moves freely ahead. The feeling no longer perpetuates itself by creating the feeler behind it."[12]

It must also be realized, and remembered, that the essential substance of the present moment is its entirety. It is not composed of just one emotional or mental or physical happening, not, for instance, just the pain you are experiencing (although the pain is of course predominant). It is also composed of everything else about you and your life that no doubt can, and in other instances, does, in varying degrees, outweigh the pain of it.

Try to find the balance. To be quite corny, try to realize and to remember that although the clouds are momentarily obscuring the sun, nevertheless the sun is there.

7 The Inferiority of Superiority

IT IS five days before Christmas, and I have stopped writing in order to trim the tree. Snow covers the deck beyond the living room. *Amahl and the Night Visitors* plays on the record player, as it has during every tree trimming for years. I am on the short stepladder, about to reach up to fix the gold star to the top of the tree.

I see I will have to go up another step, and that seems simply too high without something to hold on to for balance. "I need help," I call to Nick, who is sitting nearby watching, and commenting on, the trimming. (His part of the trimming is to get the tree firmly into the base that holds it and then to drape it with the strings of electric lights. The rest is up to me.) "I don't dare climb the ladder any higher to put the star on. Oh, look how the angel softly swings up there, as though casting blessings on the tree."

Nick got up promptly and came to stand beside the ladder, close to it. I put a hand on his shoulder to steady myself, to secure myself, and mounted the two steps carefully. Around my waist came Nick's arms—two large, sweater-warm, male arms. The warm body of this man, keeping me safe, holding me there quietly in safety. Asked to keep me safe, he stood there, happy to keep me safe. I could feel the strong quiet of his contentment in giving me safety. I could feel how he loved to be doing this.

Braced, enclosed by his arms, I stretched up to wire the star to the top of the tree.

Then there was the star, fast to the top of the tree. And Nick and I standing under it.

And now to self-concern—mine, Nick's (or rather his lack of it), other people's.

I am undoubtedly preoccupied with myself. Not as badly as I was to begin with, for I can remember way back the intensity of my preoccupation with everything about myself, particularly my appearance.

In retrospect, I see that my self-concern was excessive, that it rose rapidly, like floodwaters, during my teens and crested during my middle age and then I think (I hope) began to recede, although I am still living in its soggy aftermath. But even though it has lessened, enough of it still remains to be classified by me as "bad."

And yet how can I call something "bad" that I was born to and then led on and on into as I lived so helplessly in a childhood climate that fostered the need for concentrating excessively on myself? I can, of course, call its performance bad, and I do, even though what generated the performance was unavoidable. And so I can make allowances for badness by calling it understandable and even excusable. (I can see that this is a simplistic and an unsound concept, since through it I would have to judge and to excuse some criminality.) Nevertheless, as far as I am concerned, I can't call my preoccupation with myself deliberately bad if it was something that originally, and then on and on forever after, I really could not help and that, in an undercurrent way, I was always trying to understand and to combat. In short, the means can't be called "bad," only the end.

And I cannot possibly call bad something whose central consuming purpose was trying to figure out what the trouble was and how to be free of it. For I do think that in large part my concentration on myself is due to the mobilizing and focusing of my energies toward trying to figure out what my life is about and what, if anything, I can do about it.

It looks as though I am beginning to develop a sort of tolerance for self-concern, even a sympathy for it. It seems clear to me now that it is a universal human reaction to living with a flawed self, a self unjustly dealt with, and that the acting out of it is simply the defenses one puts up against such an unmanageable handicap.

And so I wonder whether the term "egoism"—the umbrella word for all the self-isms—really needs to imply something bad. Egoism always sounds like a nasty word, but in having to be applied to all humanity, it must, unless it is excessive, lose that implication. Perhaps there is a "normal" egoism that can be thought of as simply the habit of having to be primarily, tenaciously concerned with one's acceptance, and survival, in the conditions peculiar to one's own life.

Also, I wonder if we don't all give ourselves top priority without being conscious of doing it, knowing but not saying that our own lives matter most. And I imagine that, except for true heroes and saints and mothers, this is so.

I venture to think that moderate egoism can be thought of as neither good nor bad, and that it exists in a normal way in everyone, with as many variables as there are personalities, and that a certain degree of non-self-applauding and modest interest in oneself is a natural and a healthy thing.

Which leads me to conclude that it is only when false pride takes over, or when for whatever reason self-concern reigns dictatorially, that the word "egoism" deserves the taint it has acquired.

My self-concern is an intricate thing, I know, and I wonder whether it would be as impossible to try to isolate and analyze mine as it would be to pick apart and to analyze my entire self? Would it be a great oversimplification of the complexity of personality, background, dispositions and habits to try to comprehend and to define the relation self-concern has to all that?

Probably yes. But no matter. I must try as best I can to get the picture.

When Father wanted to wind up inconclusiveness, he always said, "Well now, let's get down to brass tacks."

Back then, that was a pretty ouchy image, and it still is, whatever it means. I presume it means that it will hurt to face the thing one must face. So, yes, I must get down to brass tacks about the specifics of my self-concern. How, specifically, do I know that I am self-concerned? What, exactly, do I feel or do that conveys to me that I am acting out self-concern? How does it reveal itself to me? How is it made known to me in terms of my feelings and my behavior?

Is it so ingrained and so habitual that I have no conscious feelings about it at all? And does it show, like the proverbial petticoat? And is it much greater than other people's? Is it above average? (As above average as my looks used to be, and in proportion to them?) I think there is a co-relation between the uses of good looks and the proliferation of self-concern and that it is even now a hindrance to a clean, aired, upward-going growth.

I'll begin with the first thing that comes to mind as an answer to my question: Why do I believe that I am abnormally self-concerned?

I believe that I am abnormally self-concerned because, when things go against me, things both large and small, it simply feels impossible, even inappropriate, that this should be happening to *me*. How could such a thing be happening to *me*, who should be exempt from adversity, protected from it?

And the next question: What exactly do I feel or do that conveys to me that I am acting out this self-concern? How does this self-concern reveal itself to me? How is it made known to me through my feelings and behavior?

The answer is that all my life I have had operating in me a monitoring mechanism that alerts me to what I know to be my own right versus my own wrong. (And I don't mean my parents' right and wrong, I mean my own innate right and wrong.) I have always known, because the phenomenon of it has been constantly operative in me, which behavior comes from integrity and feels right for me, and which comes from self-concern and feels wrong for me. I have known that integrity feels comfortable, and self-concern uncomfortable; I have known that violation of this comfort is monitored by an inner alarm, often an actual physical sensation. And so I have come to rely on the knowledge that it is natural for a part of myself to want to perpetuate what feels true to me and to resist what does not feel true.

This is the way the conflict has always gone, and still goes, with no less strength than when I was twenty: A thought, or a behavior about to be born of the thought, causes a second's hesitation, a second's pause of knowing better, or often a visceral pang along with a blush, so furiously and essentially opposed am I to what I know to be behavior that is wrong for me.

As I have this sudden foreknowledge that what I am about to say or do is going to be a far cry from the center of me that knows better, my face begins to beat with heat. "Don't say it, don't do it," or even "don't think it," this inner alarm informs me. I have actually pinpointed the most frequent self-deceptive thought I am about to speak as one that is designed to be attention-getting: Here stand I, a coin-operated machine. I put "need for acceptance" into the slot, and out comes "show-off."

Once in a while I heed the pause, I stop, I refrain from the impulsive word or action. But all the other times I struggle for a moment, or don't struggle at all, then succumb, knowing at the same time that my passive rightness has again been thwarted by my active wrongness.

I am on firm ground only when I know in my viscera, as well as in my mind, that what I am about to do or think feels wrong to me, when I am in close touch with that inner voice that is always there to be heard and to be heeded, that voice, or call it a declarative knowledge in my guts, that unmasks "performance" simply by permeating me with a sensation of futility, and often outrage, and identifies what sort of "performance" is going on.

And so that is the answer to the question at the beginning of this chapter as to whether my self-concern is so ingrained and so habitual that I have no awareness of its going on. Clearly, I have always had a pervasive awareness of its going on.

*   *   *

To sum up: First, I understand that I believe myself to be self-concerned because of an inordinate sense of my importance and value.

And second, I know that my self-concern is revealed to me through a reliable inner monitoring mechanism.

But now to the basic question: Where does this self-concern come from? Why its extremity? And why was I forced into this delusionary condition of feeling so special, as far back as I can remember?

I find two answers to this question.

For one thing, as I have suspected, feeling oneself to be special can simply be a manifestation of a perfectly normal, average self-concern—basic to everyone. Because, as I have said, every human being instinctively knows himself to be one of a kind—a specialty; instinctively, he feels that his own life is what matters most, that he is more central to his own consciousness than to any other consciousness on earth.

Or he can feel himself to be special because he has learned to need to feel that way. The conditions of his life have been such that he is in great need of inflating himself to the (spurious) posture of superiority—and the trouble is, at bottom, it does feel spurious to him. In so doing, his normal self-concern has altered and escalated into an intense concentration upon himself.

That, of course, is what happened to me. But why?

I see reasons for it right away. Among them, my missionary aunt Annie's constant glorifying praise of me: "Thou shalt give thanks, Margaret, unto the Lord, who has dealt bountifully with thee." She viewed me as a gifted child—which was an exaggeration—and proudly let it be known to everyone.

And the admiration of males—beginning in my teens.

But beneath all this—my father's thinly disguised admiration because I was the attractive child that his other two were not, and my mother's wistful awe of me because of this, along with her evident though never uttered *denial* of my right to be a bountifully-dealt-with child in the face of the deprivation of the other two. I had no tragic malformation, like theirs. Imagine the incredible good fortune of that, the desirability of it, the feeling almost of having been *chosen*. To possess physical normalcy in our family, and added to that an attractive physical normalcy—what a miracle it must have seemed, what a gift from the gods! My parents must have rejoiced at this. And was I aware of their rejoicing during the first days and weeks and months of my infant life? To be rejoiced over is to be blessed. And perhaps I was so blessed. In any event, appearance became my pride and my need and my security. Became *me*. With only a glimmer of the mind that needed to be thinking. It never occurred to me that there was anything inside my head, beneath the face I anointed every morning with cleansing cream. A head on my shoulders? I knew only one way to use what was up there on my shoulders.

There may be other areas of weakness that had to be ignored by the cover-up of self-concern, but certainly the value of appearance, imparted to me by a father whose love was all-important, was enough to establish in me an unbounded sense of superiority. Through his furtive love (its very furtiveness revealing its intensity), I came to feel like someone. I was deprived of all images of myself except his. I was Father's little Peggoty, with long, white-blond curls that he wouldn't let me cut and easy emotional tears like his and ragged fingernails that he punished me for biting.

My mother,
Helen Scott Howe

From left to right, my sister,
Helen Faxon Howe,
me, my brother,
Winthrop Keith Howe Jr.

My father, Winthrop Keith Howe

Our father-daughter-ness, though, was not as negative as that. Because I loved my father. We were, at bottom, the same. His mix was my mix, although this was unknown to both of us consciously, and it was certainly undeclared by us. We had this basic connection. Between us was a poetic sharing—for instance, the way I played a Schubert impromptu and the way he sang "Little Boy Blue"—and hearts that together saw what was in our world, though we never could or would put this into words. We never were able to tell this to each other. Perhaps we didn't have to.

To say that my alliance with my father determined my relationships with all men seems as obvious to me as to affirm that the sun rises and the sun sets, since I believe that my relation to my father was a blueprint for my marriages (as is true for a preponderance of marriages). I loved and was loved by a complexly authoritarian man, and there was nothing for it but to continue into marriage that way. His sovereignty and my willing but rebellious subjection to it became the sound and the substance of my relations with my two husbands. There is a right and there is a wrong—that to me was the absolute law of my life with my husbands. Powerlessly, I lived with the continual force of their always being right, which I felt they usually were, and of my always being wrong.

"Right and wrong, his constant song," I would say to myself in later years, with an aching forgiveness. Yet it had always been important to me to have my father's approval. It became the only way I could manage. I was his favorite, and Helen and Wint were my mother's. It was as simple and as fatal as that.

We all have this need for approval. And much of what we do is in some way motivated by it, for we don't do what we do in dissociation from other people, unless we are Robinson Crusoes. We do what we do in relation to other people and toward being perceived by them as special, beginning as infants with our mothers, or as small children with our fathers. I knew my father loved me. He told me so in many ways, and specifically in a letter he once sent me from New York when he was there on a business trip. I found it in the trunk in the attic when I was searching recently for old photographs. "I would like very much to be at home tonight and have a little girl and boy come down in their nighties and sit on my lap and then I would like to hold the wee little girl in my arms and have a little head rest down on my shoulders. You love me, don't you? Well, if you don't love me, I know I love you."

Here is a tricky question that has just surfaced in me: Precisely what is it that would go on in me if I were free to see a world not filtered by me, free to see it and to know it for what it is, not something changed by me into what it is not? What would the experience be? And what would be the reward? If I were to be taken out of my self-focus, would something occur? Does being taken out of it mean that I lose a sense of my own personality? Am I an emptied vessel, outward-directed and neuter, space-filled and euphoric, so lost without my "inward war"[13] that I have no sense of self whatsoever?

In the midst of asking myself these questions, I remembered suddenly an experience I had that seems like a good answer to them.

When I was forty-five years old, I had for a while a volunteer job in a small research project in the outpatient department of Payne Whitney Clinic in New York Hospital.

It was my job to interview the outpatients of this mental hospital and, from my layman's point of view, to write up the interviews as profiles. In conjunction with a clinician's diagnostic presentation, these reports were to be used to teach the medical students specializing in psychiatry the necessity of seeing not only patients but persons, of approaching them as human beings rather than as cases.

Wearing a starched white coat like a bona fide hospital person and feeling important in it, I met the patient I was going to interview in the waiting room and then led him or her into a small private room with two chairs and a table, where we sat down facing each other.

There was a set of questions that had to be covered, but otherwise, the interviews were open-ended, and the substance of them was up to me. I found almost immediately that my concentration was impaired if I stopped to take notes. And I found, too, that only total concentration on the person across from me enabled me to recall what he or she was or did or said. Thus, for an hour, sometimes longer, I sat with an interesting person (the patients were always of interest in some way) and had no experience but him or her. I could not interject myself in any way. I could have no reason for being there other than to be totally attentive.

And I was free to be absorbed by what was there before my eyes because, for one thing, I couldn't permit myself to be distracted by criticism. A sort of associative condemning was beside the point, since if I deviated for one minute from my exclusive concentration on, let's say, Mrs. J, if I let myself drift off into distaste for the dress that was too tight for her largeness or for the lipstick that was too purple for her lined face, if I indulged in my habit of negative judgment, then I would miss all that I was there to see and to write up, and there would be no point in this job.

What resulted, as far as I was concerned, was a miracle. In the first place, I found that I had total recall. I would hurry home and write up the interview, remembering word for word what the patient had said—if a quotation, the wording of the quotation. There was nothing new or difficult for me in remembering Mrs. J's looks and her gestures or in formulating what I felt of her beneath all this, for I have always been naturally observant. But it was the first time in my life that I had experienced total recall of spoken words. I was simply amazed by the revelation of this capacity and by the revelation of the good uses I could put my mind to if I centered completely on someone other than myself.

And my mind was freed in other ways. Inarticulate I began to talk with my friends volubly. Words didn't play hide-and-seek, they were there in my mouth. Words I didn't know I knew emerged from this unfamiliar and I must say astonishing mouth. Not only that, my thinking process was unfamiliarly clear and unimpeded and quick. I was someone else, because I was not somewhere else; I was there, in the present moment entirely. And of course the more I used my mind in this way, the more facile it became.

(Postmortem: After I stopped working on the project, I quickly lost the freedom of unself-conscious talk and reverted to my usual frustrating inarticulateness.)

That was a period during which I was more operationally connected with my nonegoistic self than I have ever been before or since, though I didn't know it at the time. I didn't experience it as freedom from egoism, only as experience.

Perhaps anyway that is the ultimate—to experience without being aware of anything but experience.

* * *

My parents taught me that I must see human beings as they should be, not as they are.

In the Payne Whitney interviews, I learned that since "freedom is what we do with what has been done to us," as Sartre says,[14] so freedom from judgments formed and cemented long ago could lead limitlessly to new, undreamed-of freedoms.

The other day I was driving along South Road and came upon two moped riders—a boy and a girl, zooming along, the boy careening showily in daring circles and swoops, the girl laughing and waving her arm encouragingly.

My instant, habitual reaction was, "That's dangerous, that's crazy, on this narrow, winding, trafficky country road. Those lobbyists and representatives in the State House in Boston who refuse to ban mopeds, they're nothing less than criminals, permitting potential murder!"

All true.

In the next second, as I continued to look at them (I had to lag behind their antics, because I didn't dare pass them on a curve), I said to myself suddenly, "But they're having such a good time."

True, too.

I was fascinated by that reaction, so absolutely new to me. Minutes later, congratulating myself that I had been able for a moment to recognize an *entirety* of what I was looking at, I had another thought, which was that there had been actual interest for me in finding, for once in that usual scene on summer roads, something other than just my rage. I was struck by the fact that a triggered, predictable response to what is there to be seen is really monotonous, boring and repetitive and, in a satiating kind of way, a waste.

Was this to be the sum of all my experiencing?
Oh no, not if I could help it.

Jon Kabat-Zinn clarified further for me the meaning and the importance of suspending judgment.

> A non-judging orientation certainly does not mean that you cease knowing how to act or behave responsibly in society, or that anything anybody does is okay. It simply means that we can act with much greater clarity in our own lives, and be more balanced, more effective, and more ethical in our activities, if we know that we are immersed in a stream of unconscious liking and disliking which screens us from the world and from the basic purity of our own being. The mind states of liking and disliking can take up permanent residency in us, unconsciously feeding addictive behaviors in all domains of life. When we are able to recognize and name the seeds of greediness or craving, however subtle, in the mind's constant wanting and pursuing of the things or results that we like, and the seeds of aversion or hatred in our rejecting or maneuvering to avoid the things we don't like, that stops us for a moment and reminds us that such forces really are at work in our own minds to one extent or another almost all the time. It's no exaggeration to say that they have a chronic, viral-like toxicity that prevents us from seeing things as they actually are and mobilizing our true potential.[15]

I am beginning to realize that an exposure to my judgmental tendencies, along with a full-fledged need to alter and to enlarge attentiveness to what is here now, could lead to an ability to view life, and myself living it, as more fact than fiction. And with some conscious new attitudes evolving hand in hand with the marvelous complexity and workings of the subconscious—what I call "the gestating gestalt"—I can finally, perhaps suddenly, one day, have an illuminating recognition of that whole, simple, sought-after Holy Grail: I can focus better, and more, on the present moment. And I can be sensible of myself in a new, true way.

I will look for fear, but I will not find it.

Paris. I am nineteen years old and newly wed. I am sitting, on a winter evening, across the table from my husband, Sam, upstairs at Fouquet's on the avenue Champs-Elysées. We have finished our dinner and the last of our wine and are addressing ourselves now to the small steaming cups of café noir that have been set down before us. I am wearing my trousseau dress of moss-green panne velvet with a green and silver lamé top. My hat, of course, is a dreadful, head-hugging cloche doing its best to defeat the young face beneath it.

Sam sets down his coffee cup. He reaches into the inner pocket of his jacket and brings out the gold cigarette case that was my wedding present to him, paid for, of course, by my parents. He presses the lid, which springs up, looks at me with an indulgent smile as he takes out a cigarette and, like the bestowal of an award or of the greatest gift, hands it meaningfully, ceremoniously across the table to me.

Oh joy! I am to be permitted a cigarette! I am ecstatic, like a dog suddenly let off a leash. (Our agreement, or rather his law to which I am obedient, has been that he will let me smoke every once in a while, but the when and the where of that must be left up to him. Father knows best.)

Sam lights the cigarette for me. Gluttonously, I inhale it. I have learned to love smoking. Sam lights his own cigarette. I draw in great drags of the head-spinning smoke, smiling hugely at my benefactor. How I love to smoke! How I long to smoke all the time. How I long to smoke whenever *I* want to; but also, how I long to have my smoking be controlled by him.

Sam was no tyrant. He was a charming, good, intelligent young man who saw his husbandly place, in the scheme of things, as dominant male. And I do not make the mistake of blaming Sam entirely for needing to be the supervising, managerial husband, since I was so slavishly collaborating with him in making him that. In a culturally conditioned way, he needed to rule me. And I, in a culturally but also more complexly conditioned way, needed to be ruled by him. Our theme song was, "I'm a little girl who's lost in the wood, I know I could, always be good, to someone who'd watch over me."[16]

It is all more complex than that, as I knew to begin with it would be. But primarily I think my exaggerated concentration on myself derived from having to be a female preoccupied to a marked degree with her body, which appeared to be what made her a winner, but who nevertheless developed a certain amount of fought-for integrity. Mine has been a self-concern resulting, I believe, chiefly from a vanity about face and form and not from other kinds of bogus self-admiration. My looks accomplished my goal successfully. And that goal, stripped to the bone, was to have the world, as my father already had, take note of me.

It took me so long, so very long, to find out why, when all was said and done, the attention I got because of my looks never satisfied me thoroughly; why it always seemed to have left something out, to increasingly make "superiority" feel so empty. It took me countless years to figure out what was wrong. A great need to be prized would seem to be the very opposite of the confidence one would expect a pride of appearance to foster.

And so just what, I had to ask myself, was this "superiority" I was flouncing around in so uncomfortably?

The answer, when it came at last, showed me that I was not in fact feeling certain, in my heart, of really being superior at all. In my heart I was not a winner, I was a loser. And what I felt superiority to be, certainly was not a legitimate self-esteem.

But if it was not self-esteem, what was it? Self-distrust?

It was self-distrust. It was a great uncertainty. Thanks to some native honesty, I did at bottom think very poorly of my razzle-dazzle self-promotion, though I was obliged for this reason, contradictorily, to sell myself as other than this, as desirable, special, important, and so on. In trying to feel superior, I was simply trying to prove that I was not inferior.

Yes. The initial confidence and euphoria about being prized for my looks had gradually been infiltrated and displaced by a growing understanding that something vital and essential was being ignored. And all the time, at bottom what I really craved was to be recognized not primarily for my appearance but profoundly and longingly, even pathetically, for something in me that knew better—my mind, my true spirit, my integrity—that part of me that had had such a hard time seeing the light of day.

Needless to say, neither the narcissism nor the deep deprivation of having no one in the world know me for what I was under my skin, was a solid base for good growth. And the result of these two forces was my expanding and great uncertainty about who this little girl really was who lived so helplessly and so longingly for the attention of others.

The ingredients of fear were accumulating.

If this concern with self-concern has all sounded like an exhaustive, never-ending pursuit of perfection, I can only say that it should be apparent what one has to contend with in this world, in trying to keep alive the elusive potential for vision and peace. Someone once asked me, years ago, why I sought perfection so intensely. I was surprised at the question, because it seemed evident to me that my search was not for perfection but was simply for finding ways in which to be natural.

Of course, to expect perfection is unrealistic and perhaps, egoism being one of the enemies I must fight, in itself egoistic, as perfectionism surely can be. And I see now that I have also sought a kind of perfection unrelated to the voice of integrity. Plus I am not only that kind of precarious perfectionist but alas also a puritan (perhaps they are the same thing), which certainly confuses the issue, so that it often seems, even to me, that I am impossibly striving for the perfect life lived by the perfect person. Yet what I actually am is a puritanized perfectionist and at the same time, contradictorily, a seeker after my own truth.

Self-concern? Integrity? Is the writing of this book in part self-concern declaring the invalidity of itself, and in part (we shall see) a desire for integrity declaring the validity of itself? Or more likely, is it a combination of both?

*   *   *

Nick sometimes teaches me by example. For instance, one day last summer we had a conversation that demonstrated my self-concern and his lack of it. We were sitting on the front deck, enjoying the sun and the air that were helping Nick recover from a major abdominal operation. The awning over the deck snapped softly in the warm wind coming across the pond from the sea. The sun beat down on the smell of hot canvas. Beneath it we sat. I held in both my hands a card to Nick from Tamara about his illness, which he had just finished reading and, without a word, had handed over to me to read. It was a large piece of folded, stiff green paper, on the front of it a cutout of four red hearts and underneath, Tamara's words:

> To my dearest, most stubborn, and most beloved Grandfather. I've been thinking about what I wanted to tell you and what you might want to or not want to hear. I don't know and can't know your thoughts, but being just as strongminded as you, I'm going to tell you mine anyway.
>
> Mostly I just want you to really know that for better or worse I adore you. You are my only grandfather. Someone I was a little scared of and in awe of when younger, but who I later found I could challenge and debate with and explore what I was learning in life. And then after that, someone who I learned to respect and value in a way I never have with anyone else. Someone who I knew really cared about me and was completely direct, "cut to the chase," and honest. You and Gran have been a sounding board, a center, and the place I go—literally or in my mind—when I need to retreat, be calm and feel loved. This will never change for me whether you die before you

get this letter, or in 20 years, whether you die by some method of your choice or by time, whether my last memory of you is reading the *Economist* or being fed puréed beef stew. It's just the way it is.

I miss you and would like to come see you and Gran—you could always shut your door, and I can fix my own gin and tonic—but I'd love to say hello.

At risk of sounding like a high school year book—love always. Tamara

I folded the card and looked at the red hearts on the front of it, which blurred. "This," I said, and my voice broke, "is a wonderful, wonderful thing." I handed the card back to him.

He took it calmly. No movement of Nick's is ever abrupt, or slow, but always calmly and strongly spaced. And that is the way he reached out his hand for the card, and took it from me, and put it back down on the driftwood table in front of our chairs.

After a while he said, evenly, "Yes. It is one of the most wonderful things that has ever happened to me in my life."

I was stunned by Nick's saying something directly and unguardedly from his heart. I had only heard him say anything of the sort once before in our life together, when, in the kitchen one day doing something at the counter, he had said abruptly and fiercely, not to me, but to the counter, "You're the best thing that ever happened to me in my life." I didn't know then, and I don't know now, where that came from or why. But I have hoarded it.

And now, once again, this secret man had opened. I knew a happiness for him that was vast and certain. I looked at him, who was the center of my life, and a compass for Tamara's.

Then, without plan, something I had to say to him came out: "Nick, I wish you could *use* this love Tamara has for you. I mean, I wish you could, well, incorporate it. Let it give you a life of knowing yourself for what you are, knowing you are what *she* knows you are, and let it fill you out, let it, well, buck you up. If I were to be told about myself the things Tamara told you, I would be so, well, *reassured* about myself. I could say to myself, am I really like that? And if I am, why do I have such self-doubt that I'm not? I could take it into me, and keep it there, and fall back on it. It would add to me. I wish you could—oh, not just from Tamara, but from the other people who love and respect and admire you—could *use* this. Maybe I mean, could just *believe* this about yourself. I think you simply don't know what a remarkable man you are. Oh, I wish you'd *use* this letter, I do so wish you would."

It was a long time, it must have been five minutes, before he spoke. And then, "I don't feel the need of it," was all he said. He looked ahead of him, out to the sea.

8 The Need to be Whole

CHRISTMAS is over. It was nice, particularly the tree. Only the tree, for that matter, since the gift part of Christmas, which I have lost zest for, is only a tiring obligation to me now. I've lost interest in objects. I'm at the stage of life where I want to get rid of things rather than acquire them.

Books I love to get and to give. But otherwise, the buying and wrapping and giving of objects at Christmas is something I'm not vibrantly involved in anymore; and even getting objects, though I have a love for the giver and a gratitude for what the giver feels for me, usually doesn't inspire more than a halfhearted thank you.

However. The gift to end all gifts! This Christmas Nick gave me two life-sized small deer made out of straw—a stag and a doe. We took them out to the lawn beside the house and staked them to the ground, side by side in front of the Russian olive trees that thrash in the sea wind. From a distance you can't tell they aren't real deer.

Right away I saw that they were Nick and Peggy, put out to pasture, grazing companionably and inseparably together in the last years of their lives.

* * *

The Stag and the Doe

> As far as the stars are from the earth, and as different as fire is from water, so much do self-interest and integrity differ.
>
> —Lucan, *Pharsalia* VIII. l. xv

Integrity is a word I use all the time, but without ever having actually cracked the nut to find the meat, though of course I know that in a thing, being integrated is to be one, not two or more elements, and in a person, it is not being two or more contradictory persons but one single one. And I know some cliché synonyms for lack of it, all accurate:

My mind is blown
I am falling apart
I must pull myself together
I am at sixes and sevens
I must get it together
I am coming to my senses
I went to pieces

My therapist explained integrity well in a conversation we had about why it appealed so greatly to me and why I so longed for it for myself.

> Me: What is the inspiration of integrity?
>
> M.B-G.: Why does anyone want to be all of a piece?
>
> Me: That's my question. What came before my exposure to my father, whose integrity has always been my inspiration?
>
> M.B-G.: No. Don't in this case talk just about your father. This I believe to be an evolutionary matter that is probably true for every organism—it seeks to be wholly what it is quite naturally, what it has been programmed

to be, requiring the sun and the water to make it really happen. But, oppositely, when you're flying apart sort of centrifugally in all directions, then you're in pain and you're not growing.

Me: In other words, that's just a natural thing for any organism—to want to be whole.

M.B-G.: For any organism, its own growth demands that it develop in such a way that it is a whole. The wish to get it together is a universal wish that we are really born with, every organism is born with it—not that a flower has a conscious wish to get it together, but a flower needs to develop according to its own nature, and in such a way that it is a whole flower, a perfect flower or as near perfect as it can get.

Me: This is an innate thing, then? That "all things long to persist in their being?"[17]

M.B-G.: I think so. I think it's innate in all organisms.

Me: It would have to be innate, obviously, if you're talking about flowers.

M.B-G.: That's what has kept life going. The innate necessity of an organism to come out in one piece. It's remarkable how few aberrations there are—like Siamese twins or people born with a mouth in their forehead or whatever. It doesn't make for the survival of the flower if it doesn't get it together. It doesn't make for the continuity of the species, either.

Me: Well, could you say, then, that from the beginning I was mostly ignorant and confused about what the perfect flower was, but at the same time, I knew exactly what it was and I wanted to be it? That my inner alarm system never let me forget it?

M.B-G.: Yes. I would say just that.

My response to this was instantaneous and absolute, bringing to light my own innate knowledge of integrity, which from the time I was a small child who loved country fields has always exemplified the very same thing I then sensed and believed the natural world to be. I mean that although I didn't know it in so many words, from the very beginning, nature was integrity to me. Look at me, the fields of daisies said. Child and flower are the same.

There is a photograph of me at the age of two—white organdy dress with ribbon rosettes and lace inserts, white stockings wrinkled over fat little ankles, white strap slippers with bows. I am standing stiffly beside a low chair on which there is an open picture book, my hands resting unnaturally on it with fingers prissed up into curves, probably arranged that way by the anxious photographer. My forehead is shortened by bangs, and there are sausage curls alongside my cheeks. My eyes dominate—large and dark and angry-sad. My disbelieving, unaccommodating, not quite sullen mouth goes slightly down at the corners.

A photograph of a bewildered and frightened child, wherein contradictory forces had begun to muddle the two-year-old integrity that was struggling to become the perfect flower. They were potent, these forces. They were omnipotent. What anxious battles this child had to deal with in this world of picture books that were not for looking at but for artificially placed hands to be displayed on.

Ah! Now I see the connection between integrity and fear. Or rather, the disconnection:

The little girl in the photograph is obviously composed

Me, at two

of warring forces—her own dos and other people's don'ts. With an innocent trust that Father and Mother know best, and everyone else, too, she is already complexly split, full of crevices. She is all apart inside, not together, afraid all the time. And she doesn't yet know how to develop anything cohesive to hold her securely together inside and to keep her from being always frightened. Because being split apart hurts. The seesaw of her short life so far has been its duality—failure and promise, hide and seek, having to pretend that the picture book is not for looking at (which she knows it is for) but for posing prissy fingers on—the embattled coexistence in her of the struggle of her own dos (integrity) versus her parents' and society's don'ts (the adversary of integrity).

Will there ever come into her being an impermeable glue to hold her together? No crevices that hurt? Will she ever be able to stand strong in a storm (old age) and not be dissolved in it? Will she ever, with so much against her, come close to being the perfect flower?

I have an unshakable conviction that the potential for integrity existed in that little girl. And that it exists in everyone in some degree. I also believe that no one on this earth with a strong and persistent capacity for integrity ever totally loses his comprehension of this capacity, which is so vital to his best development, no matter how much of an egoist he becomes, no matter how much or how often he fails himself—Gandhi's principle of the best in oneself.

I know that my struggle for integrity is as lively now as it was in that little girl in the photograph. Oh, I think much livelier. For time is running out. I am not that child anymore (except that in some ways I am, and that is part of the trouble). No. I am a woman growing very old and I am afraid of being afraid. I would like to find out what it feels like to be unafraid, or as near to that state as I can get.

I have had a period of durable joy, which comes, I believe, from the satisfaction of all this thinking about integrity.

Yesterday, as I was driving along Middle Road, suddenly the world, everything I saw in it, exploded, scintillated. It was as though my body, interchangeable with the sun-lighted world, was at a high boil. The sky was clear blue. The sea, beyond the sheep pasture sloping down to it, was an infinite spread of incandescent blueness. The pond, behind the dunes separating it from the sea, was so startling in its deepness and darkness of blue that I wondered how water separated by only a few feet of beach could be so different in color.

At that moment, my capacity for joy felt limitless. What is it in me that can ever deny this, I wondered? But I knew. I knew that it was impossible for me to live at such a soaring pitch day in, day out. Too many variables.

Among them, as I was learning, all my self-isms. What a drag they are. And what a high I can be on when I begin to come up from darkness into the open air and see; and know what truth is and what it is not.

When I got back home, everything I did, I did with a bounce, a spring in my step, a lightness and a lengthening of my striding body, which felt as long and as stretched limberly up as Alice in Wonderland grown tall. Long-necked Alice strode down the long hall on the worn Iraqi rug, and even though my neck seemed to reach to the ceiling, I could still bend it and see the birds and faces in the rug.

And then, sitting at the lunch table, I picked up my glasses and gazed out the window for a long time at the squirrel, the one with the wispy tail, wrapped around the bird feeder on the deck. "Now he's been replaced by the one with the bushy tail," I said to Nick. Who said after a moment, "The wispy-tailed one is always chasing the other away."

"Perhaps the wispy-tailed one is aggressive because of the handicap of his wispy tail," I said. And then I picked a crumb from the front of my sweater, marveling that this should be of interest.

Still (and I groan, because I thought I had it all wrapped up), I am held back by a nagging, perplexed sense of not having really gotten to the bottom of what I'm trying to find out.

Because I now feel that there must be some generative force that lies underneath, for example, the push for integrity. Something that begets integrity and causes it to work, something capable of permitting or enabling the endeavor of integrity. Something that can be called the essence of myself? The best of myself (not in a moralistic way, but in a life-giving way)? Something I see, imagistically, as a small area that lies at my center and ticks away, often loudly, often inaudibly, as from day to day I ponder the puzzles and the fears of old age?

This is the question that is at the very root of the profound problems of my fears about old age. And frankly, I suppose there is no simple answer to it. Because how impossible it is, for a nonprofessional like me, to attempt in a scholarly way to define the complexities and contradictions of the human psyche.

It is not simple to understand human behavior. There is no one thing that accounts for the growth or the withering of the spirit. Nevertheless, as I have said, I am attracted to the concept of a central, isolated, unquenchable entity that lies underneath everything else and that gives origin to it.

Thirteen years ago, crossing the Atlantic on the *Cristoforo Colombo*, I wrote about this very thing, not realizing then that what I was exploring was at the very heart of the self-definition I'm exploring in my writing. I am pleased to realize that today's search is really a reembarkation on a theme not new to me, even though it had to wait almost a decade and a half to develop in a way that brought everything else into focus.

In this foreign country of losses both great and small, it is good to know that there is one thing not lost to me, perhaps never lost, and that is the will to have some kind of inner continuance, some ongoing thing that seems to remain when all else appears to be lost.

I was all by myself on that voyage from France to New York on the *Cristoforo Colombo*. Nick had had to fly back suddenly because of business, and I was scared of flying then, so I took the boat we had planned to come back on together.

Being shy, I kept to myself the whole trip, though I would have liked to meet someone to have drinks with before lunch and dinner. All I did for six days was eat and sleep and walk the deck and think and write. I never in my life slept so much and so refreshingly for an entire week as I did on that trip. And it wasn't a torpid sleep at all. On the contrary. Two hours after lunch, plus eight, nine hours each night, was not sluggish-making sleep, but energizing. I remember being astonished at how rested, even, yes, more youthful my face had begun to be. One day this fresh-faced woman looked back at me from the mirror, and I sat there marveling at what sleep could accomplish.

When I wasn't sleeping, I walked the deck, I sat in my deck chair, or I sat on the bed in the cabin looking out of the porthole at the heaving sea, and I thought, I made notes, I wrote. I did almost nothing else except drink sherry before lunch and vermouth before dinner in the bar and eat a long, elaborate Italian dinner solitarily (I had requested a table for one) in the slowly-tipping-from-side-to-side vast dining room.

My entire self, it seemed, was sharpened and focused on thinking, due, I suppose, to solitude and rest and concentration, and of course to the perspective gained from being away from home, on a trip, and in limbo as one can be only on a ship at sea. Revved up to this new adventure of concentrated thinking, I couldn't let it go for one minute, except in sleep, and obviously not even there, for I had many and vivid dreams. This is what I wrote:

> The past has meaning only insofar as I have lived it, in one way or another, up to now. But all my moments of deepest experiencing have shown me that only the very present is totally alive, and that therefore the past is not alive in the sense of complete participation.
>
> Up until just before this moment, the past is myself as I was. From this moment on and for its duration, this present is a combination of myself as I WAS and as I AM.
>
> Here, at the beginning of this moment, everything I feel, or do, or think, or say, is a result of the past. At the

onset of this moment, I am about to feel, or act, from out of my ancestral and environmental past. In terms of experience, I exist now because of my past existence.

But as a combination composed of heredity and environment, within that mix and fundamentally exclusive of environmental influences, is a thing I call I AM, something that is fixed, constant, unchanging, as opposed to all else that is flowing, temporal.

Independent and rooted and steadfast as this I AM is, still I am more likely to be and to act, from out of the totality of past and present, and also from out of presentiments and projections of the future, rather than from out of that solitary, faint, often barely alive, present I AM.

I see that I AM has a twofold meaning. It means, obviously, that I, this total woman, am alive and functioning in this present. I live, I breathe, I think, *I am* alive. But it means, as well, that within that totality, and an independent part of it, is something else, something different from all the rest of the totality, which is I AM. The present moment is not *wholly* apparent to any part of me except to this independent entity.

I am trying to say that I am finding out I am two things—a cumulative conglomerate of a hereditary and environmental past, plus a single, constant present, which is always in the passage of the past, and will continue to be in the passage of the future.

A statement of William James that I came upon a few weeks ago casts a new and further light on my own concepts of a separate I. I include it because it is a theory that anyone interested in self-identity might want to think about and pursue.

> Whatever I may be thinking of, I am always at the same time more or less aware of *myself*, of my *personal existence*. At the same time it is *I* who am aware; so that the total self of me, being as it is duplex, partly known and partly knower, partly object and partly subject, must have two aspects discriminated in it, of which for shortness we may call one the *me*, and the other the *I*. The *I*, or "pure ego," is a very much more difficult subject of inquiry than the *me*. It is that which at any moment is conscious, whereas the *me* is only one of the things which it is conscious of. In other words, the *I* is the *thinker*.[18]

In summing up those theories of mine thirteen years ago, I wrote:

> If I can operate better without the encumbrances of the past or the imaginings of the future, and if living in the here and now is the key to the fullest, surest way of being, then couldn't experience be more constant and true if I AM were more in control, since I wouldn't be viewing the world largely through the flux, and so often, the behavioral and experiential hang-ups of the past or, through the unverifiable imaginings of the future, but rather to a greater extent through the uninfluenced, constant, fixed eye of I AM. Would I cease to be so much composed of the experiences of the past, which are my only models for present and future behavior—particularly the unrealities of fears and insufficiencies and pretensions—if I were more in touch with the fixed constant of I AM?

As I have been discovering, looking forward to SOMETHING ELSE is totally unrealistic, is a mirage, since how can I possibly know what the imagined experiences will be? All I do know is that in conceiving of that future experience I am only reiterating past experience, or even present experience, obviously my only models for future experience. Though to suggest that new experience is related only to the future is misleading. Because it is obviously only in the present that I am having experience old or new, and only in the moment that I am reexperiencing I AM, or experiencing what is outside of that self, or both.

Alan Watts says:

> Tomorrow and plans for tomorrow can have no significance at all unless you are in full contact with the reality of the present, since it is in the present and *only* in the present, that you live. There is no other reality than present reality, so that, even if one were to live for endless ages, to live for the future would be to miss the point entirely.[19]

9 Self-Concern is Fear

THE STAG and the doe are not standing up to winter, the severest in years. The doe is not, in fact, weathering it. Her head is coming apart. (It's hard for me not to take this as a metaphor for mine.) I have tried to bind her disintegrating straw muzzle, first with invisible thin fishing line, which didn't work, then with clear wide plastic tape, which, at a distance, did. But even from a distance, she has exactly the look of a shapeless creature who is old and can't do anything about it and doesn't care—a perishable old female.

The stag still stands upright, head high and fixed, even though one of his forelegs is beginning to buckle.

I care, though, about those two. I look at them every day and know that their deterioration is now irreversible.

They are going.

But before they are really gone, we will have to give them the dignity of some kind of disappearance that feels all right to us (meaning to me, for Nick doesn't play this game).

What will that disappearance be?

* * *

I believe I now understand the great part that self-concern plays in my fear of old age. For one thing, fearfully, I anticipate the loss of that "attractive physical perfection" that has always been my dominant sense of what I am and what I am for—the paramount part of my self-identity, and not in any possible way expressive of that innate search for the perfect flower, which I began my life with and have tried persistently and imperfectly to nurture.

Old age promises to rob me, too, of all those self-isms I took for granted as being a sure self-identity, but which now are declaring themselves to be unreliable and perishable. Among them, I am beginning to be uneasy about the overwrought need I have for a man, the compulsion to have my life be defined by a man, to have my self be subject to him. In the meantime, my tiny little budding integrity has not yet become a force dominant enough to fill the growing vacuum. And so old age looms fearfully as a wasteland in which a fading surety is fast departing and in which there is as yet no true new surety either, in fact, no surety at all.

What I am finding out about extreme self-concern—mine, perhaps everyone's—and am trying to say about it is that to be living with an intense concentration upon oneself is to be living with what, essentially, one is not; it is to be held back from what one could be. It is to be living with all the promise of one's potential that has never had a chance to bloom. It is to be living with the failure of the flower.

This is the great part self-concern plays in the fear of old age, and it is a universal fear not solely, of course, having to do with the loss of youthful looks. It is the fear of losing the counterfeit superiorities and dependencies that have been so largely all one has ever had, and of having nothing substantial to take the place of them. It is knowing that any extreme self-ism is an imprisoning thing, like a stationary place—a place of old, squirrel-cage habit, fenced in, barricaded against the possibility that much good might move into it or out of it.

And overall, inherent in self-concern is fear itself. For self-concern *is* fear. Fear is an underlying consumer of time and energy and emotion and surely demands a more intense concentration upon oneself than almost anything else. It is impossible to have one's self be acutely primary without having fear be a fixed condition. The strain of being a highly competitive creature is great. It is hard, worrisome work, a debilitating occupation, to be always engaged in high-gear approval-seeking. Combat may seem too strong a word, but then, whether one is conscious of it or not, all competition is combat of one degree or another. One's tensions attest to this.

In his journals, John Cheever says, "The energy and the vigor of anxiety may fill a life with activity and invention, but it is an egocentric performance."[20]

And, I may add, a fear-ful one.

And so, at this point in my search, I realize that my self-concern, even if it is gradually receding, is still something that gets in my way and that only now, in my old age, have I begun to be aware of it and to realize its peril. Fears of growing old have finally and forcibly brought to my attention how perishable my counterfeit female superiority and dependencies have been, what baseless grounds I have for them, and how obstructionist they have been and still are to the pursuit of a reassuring answer to that question: If there is an inner woman there, other than the woman I see in the mirror, who is that woman?

10 Putting My Mind to It

EXCEPT FOR two short-lived instances when I was a teenager, there had never been any way for me to know, as I hope I have explained, that I had a mind needing to be used and that I would be capable of using it.

And so it is easy to see why what school was for had no interest for me and why I was a continual failure in it. My parents were always in despair because of threats to expel me for my dreamy uninvolvement and my awful marks and the reports that were continually hand written on my report cards: "Margaret has a good mind but she will not apply herself." I can't imagine why I *wasn't* expelled.

When I was fifteen, I met Miss Theodora Cummins. She was an Englishwoman who taught diction and language at the Eastman School of Music, and through my sister's music teacher there, Mother heard about her and engaged her to tutor me in French so that I might have some hope of passing the entrance exams for the boarding school I was provisionally enrolled in.

Miss Cummins was religiously and relentlessly single-minded: "You are here to learn French, and French you will of course learn." She was, in fact, a slave driver, and it was clear to me right away that she wouldn't tolerate a pupil who refused to study.

And so, in perplexity and in fear, sensing that there was no alternative, I began to give Miss Cummins my attention; I took home pages and pages of homework (really overlong assignments) and astonished my parents and myself by doing them—with difficulty and loud complaints, but conscientiously.

Theodora Cummins had great, beautiful, sad gray eyes and a British accent, which was glamorous, because only actresses and duchesses had British accents. She was also an "old maid." When she wasn't leaning over me with breath that smelled of Listerine, hammering the open textbook with her bumpy, twisted arthritic finger, *making* me pay attention, *making* me do it right, *telling* me that I *could* do it right, when she wasn't being a slave driver but could sit back and be approving of what I had accomplished, then she could smile, sadly, and look really beautiful in spite of being an "old maid" with deep wrinkles in her sad face.

At first, real study was of course the hardest thing I had ever done in my life. But within a few weeks I was at it with a grudging vigor, generated by a sound fear of not doing it and by a fascination with this whole new inviting thing I was being forced into and was actually succeeding in.

I began to worship Miss Cummins as much as I feared her. She had made me know I had a mind—the first person ever to do that.

When I got to boarding school, the newness and strangeness, the challenges and terrors and temptations and excitement of it caused me to slide back easily into my old habits of "not applying my mind." I daydreamed in class; in study hall, covertly I wrote love poems in my notebooks or designed clothes for Q. B. Jackson to make or made lists of boys I thought I might want to fall in love with. I had, though, somewhere in me, begun to realize that almost everyone else except me in this school took it seriously, particularly the awesome "old girls." And I had, too, entered into a new place of being "someone" by my election to the glee club, where I began to love the discipline, and my accomplishment through it of singing alto parts in successful countervoice.

But aside from these little stirrings toward being a responsible student, for the most part, as usual, I avoided seriousness. I was given warnings by my teachers that I was heading into something I would be sorry for, but I was simply unable to want to do anything else but what I so comfortably and mindlessly was doing.

At the beginning of November, I was summoned to the office of Miss Dangerfield, the dean.

I had never encountered such an awesome power in such a tiny person—huge power all compressed into such smallness, maybe like Queen Victoria. She terrified me. I hated that power. She pointed to a chair near her desk and told me to sit down, flipped open decisively a folder that contained my academic report and spoke, looking down at it and then up and across to me with level, resolute, pitiless eyes.

"Your marks for this first semester, Margaret, are unacceptable to this school. I see here a D in mathematics, and E in history, a C-minus in Latin, a C in geometry, a, well, B in English, yes there is some indication of application there, and in French, too, a B-plus. But *some* application to these two subjects does not outweigh the entire lack of it in the other four. I'm afraid I must tell you that unless all your marks come up to the academic minimum requirements of this school in the next semester, you will not be permitted to return to it at the end of that time. I have written your parents to this effect. We believe you have a good mind, Margaret. We also know you refuse, for reasons of your own, to apply it.

"Now, then. What we have decided to do is this. We are moving you this weekend to a single room, where you will not have the distraction of your roommates and can better apply yourself to study. It is only down the hall from them," more kindly, "so you won't feel entirely separated from them.

"There are now three weeks until the Thanksgiving recess. After that, there are three weeks until the Christmas vacation. So you have six weeks in which to demonstrate your intentions and your capacities. We don't expect an overnight improvement, Margaret, of course. But what we do expect, what we demand here, is effort. You know the Dobbs motto, Margaret: 'Do it with thy might.' That's what we expect from you, what we believe you can give, and quite frankly, what you must give in order to remain here." Again kindly now, even gently, "Is that clear, Margaret?"

I did not speak.

"I know this is sudden, Margaret. But I think you can face it. In fact, I'm rather confident you can. It is your opportunity for growth, my dear, and some day you will be grateful for it. And, well, if you are not prepared to make the effort to prove yourself capable of it, then we have overestimated you."

Almost immediately, a counterforce flared in me that would not allow the consequence just described, that would fight such failure and disgrace; a counterforce, furthermore, embellished with pride by this manifest faith in my capacities. I was almost flattered, and stopped hating her.

Could I do it? Did I want to do it?

Yes, I could do it. Miss Cummins had shown me that. And did I want to do it? Oh yes. This serious place, these serious "old girls," the little pinnacle on which I now stood as "someone" in the serious singing of alto parts, all told me that I wanted to do it and could do it. Even, yes, longed to do it.

I stood up. "I will try," I faltered. "Honestly, I will try. I can do it, Miss Dangerfield."

So moved was I by my own perfection that I burst into a flood of tears and fled.

The part of me that wanted to be, and could be, adult; the discipline; the recognition of certain basic, unalterable facts that one had to deal with in order to be adult—all this, like tiny embryonic pinkish spring leaves on bare branches, began to unfold in me almost overnight. Hiding in me, waiting for its chance, seventeen-year-old budding maturity stepped out in the light and took over.

In class, with new effort, I did what came surprisingly and interestingly easy to me—I listened; I thought. Yes. I could think. It was quite possible to think, as with Miss Cummins it had been. But it was very hard. Harder than daydreaming. Though by being so very hard, it was almost more fun than daydreaming.

I began to learn.

Then I began to love learning.

At last I understood, I felt, throughout myself, what a "mind" was, what it could mean. The quiet of the library was a quiet that hummed with the working of minds and with a silence insistently, richly palpitant with all the life in all the books on its shelves. Lying on my stomach on the cold floor of my single room, for two hours every evening I studied. I did nothing but study. I solved geometry problems in my sleep, or rather I woke up with the answers to problems I had tackled and been unable to solve before going to sleep. My mind was almost all there was. And I loved being almost entirely all mind. It was the firmest ground I had ever been on. It felt right for me. Much more right than being almost entirely emotional.

June.

Class Day.

The chapel was packed with students and parents, the faculty in cap and gown were seated on the platform. Summer sun slanted through the ruby and cobalt and honey-gold of stained glass.

Miss Dangerfield stepped up to the podium to announce the "winners" of the graduating class.

She distributed the honors, the awards, to those fortunate few who rose in a storm of applause and made their stunned, proud, applauded way up to the stage.

With pseudogenerosity but with jealousy, I joined in the extravagant hand clapping, though I was crushed when the award giving seemed over and I had not gotten anything. All my Spartan effort felt, at this moment, to have been for nothing. Deflated, diminished, disliking the ignominious position of a loser, I was in fact crushed. Had I really expected a prize? If pinned down, I would not have known *what* prize, but yes, I had hoped for a prize.

The applause died away. The audience waited. There was silence while Miss Dangerfield lowered her eyes to the papers on the podium.

She looked up. "I have the following special award to announce." Pause. "It is my pleasure to announce today that Margaret Howe has won the E.S.L. Outstanding Effort Award. It is a recognition for special effort and achievement, and one we do not bestow *every* year, for it is not every year that we have a student who is in the special position of having to make the choice 'to sink or to swim,' as the saying goes. But this year, we have such a student. Margaret Howe did what some of us on the faculty thought, frankly, might be the impossible. After a faltering start to the school year, her marks rose steadily and quite remarkably, enough to allow her to enroll for the college preparatory curriculum. We of the faculty feel that hers has been a dedicated academic and personal performance. Our pride and congratulations go to Margaret Howe, who 'Did it with her might.'"

The applause has never stopped echoing in my ears.

Even now, I never fail to cry when I think about Class Day and that moment that was the pinnacle of my life. It mattered so much to me that I had been given recognition *for the use of my mind.* It mattered more than anything else ever had (except for the publication of my books). And now, years later, I always weep for letting it all go so soon after graduation and for not going to college because I wanted to get married. Marriage! The best use of my mind had no place in that scheme of things.

It was only through writing that I found my mind again, after marrying Nick; but even then, I was never able to make the best use of it beyond the four walls of my study. It saddens me that I did not go to college, where, possibly (but who knows?), I might have continued on in the discipline forced on me by Miss Cummins and Miss Dangerfield and, in so doing, developed more lastingly the habit of thinking.

No wonder, then, that the discovery, at last, of the absolute necessity of using my mind in the entire way it was meant to be used has surfaced as so vital to my continuance and, actually, so vital to the understanding and the management of fear. For I think I do see now that the intensity of my fear comes from not having taken hold of my life with the mind that was given to me for that purpose.

> And now I am trying to master the Hell in my life, to bring all the darkness into the light. It is time, high time, that I grew up.
>
> "How does one grow up?" I asked a friend the other day. There was a slight pause; then she answered, "By thinking."
>
> —May Sarton[21]

It wasn't until years later—until recently, in fact, while reading parts of a book on Buddhist thought and doctrine and coming upon an arresting principle about the mind—that I was ready for its concept. Instantly I seized upon it, and it has stayed with me, grown in me, and been totally accepted by me as the basic formula for self-mastery through the use and the development of the mind. It has enabled me to see at last what it has taken me so long to fully grasp and to act upon: that "mind precedes things, dominates them, creates them."[22]

* * *

This Buddhist doctrine of the mind teaches three things:

> *To know the mind*—that is so near to us, and yet so unknown.
>
> *To shape the mind*—that is so unwieldy and so obstinate, and yet may turn pliant.
>
> *To free the mind*—that is in bondage all over, and yet may win freedom here and now.[23]

A year ago, these rules would have seemed to me merely abstractions—discouragingly like signposts are to foreign travelers—unarrived at and therefore unexperienced places that may become real but are at the moment only names, only the promise of what the traveler is heading toward.

But now, at this stage in my journey, I see that everything I have written so far leads me to this obvious and practical theory of self-mastery, and that everything from now on will, I believe, validate and expand its logic and its value and its all-encompassing enablement.

The three steps of the uses of the mind are listed in their logically achievable order.

The first step is to know the mind. Since I have spent many, many years trying to know my mind through self-inspection, through writing, and through professional guidance, this rule for trying to become wise doesn't stagger me as it once would have. But it goes without saying that the causes of buried and unnamed disturbances within anyone have to be unearthed and brought to light before they can be truthfully assessed and dealt with. To become a willfully thinking person in any onward way, having all along developed a background of subliminal receptivity and resolution, it is necessary to have some kind of ongoing, dynamic self-knowledge.

I have had in recent years the unequaled good fortune to be in a moderate (as opposed to an intense) therapy—a once-a-month, not-delving-deep-into-dreams, not-lying-on-the-couch kind—with a woman whose skill is equal to a heart the size of this terrestrial globe (for the preservation of which she often, literally, lays her life on the line). Skill and heart combined are what I have been the lucky recipient of in my relation to her.

She has led me to an understanding, a "knowing," of the powerful childhood imprint on me of the terror resulting from the family circumstance—the dominant one, which is nevertheless ineradicable for having been unintentional—that permeated and ruled with a tangled fear my life from childhood on. Not a starkly clear-cut, simple fear but an intricate fear slippery with contradictoriness. I will never lose it entirely, I know. The most I can hope to do is to bring reason to bear on its senseless recurrence, to think about it, to separate the fearful fantasies of the worst that could happen from the facts of what is actually happening—in my family, the worst *had* happened and thereafter became for us all an immutable law of prophecy.

As of this day, through my therapy, the "knowing" about the reasons for my early childhood terrors is complete, it is vivid and all there, ready to go, you might say, ready to be translated into "doing."

And my therapist's belief in creativity, specifically (for me) in writing, has been one of her contributions to, goads to, my struggle for integrity—my "effort to synthesize the incompatibilities steadily seeking union within me. . . . When he had managed creatively to solve his personal crisis of identity . . . and to establish a cohesive, 'one-pointed' unity with the diversities of himself, he experienced a joyous 'coming together' and, at the same time, an unprecedented freedom."[24]

My writing has always been one of the paths toward that freedom, though it took my therapist to convince me that it was not the self-indulgence of a woman of leisure but a valuable self-therapy that was my way of finding out what I was absolutely unaware of knowing. It has been the most powerful unaided implement for revealing to my surprised self a buried mine of disclosures. It has been the means whereby I discover, and release, more knowing than I had any idea I had. (All people know a lot more than they think they do!) Writing, for me, has always been a search, a sense of ongoingness, a sense of not standing still. I recommend it to anyone who can hold a pencil or use a typewriter or speak into a tape recorder.

The second step is to shape the mind. At the beginning of this thinking/writing project, I wouldn't have had the foggiest idea of how to go about "shaping" my mind or even how to begin to grasp what it is like to have a "shaped" mind or what the consequences of that would be.

However, at this point in my search, I am able to assume that "shaping" the mind will be a thought process that develops as self-knowledge progresses. The guiding base of it will be "knowing," which in turn, through the conscious "shaping" of the mind backed by the gestating gestalt, will eventually become "doing." I believe that it will have to be, among other things, a disciplinary process, a constant self-reminder to stop, to look, to listen. To think. To act.

I also believe that "shaping" will be, for me, the toughest of the two endeavors, because I have never been able to shape "knowing" into "doing," have never had the ability to "do" what I tell myself I must "do."

Now, though, in my old age, I see that there is not always tomorrow, and that if my last years are to be well lived, I *must* develop the ability to "do" as well as to "know," and that "I myself must mix with action, lest I wither by despair."[25] What's more, I realize that I am ardently looking for rescue from that interminable stalemate, and even have a kind of faith that at last a lifetime of puzzling emotional paralysis is about to be tackled and dealt with.

Quite simply, I must proceed to use my mind. I must, really, make a heroic effort to *think*, in all circumstances that require thought, and always in counterbalance to obfuscating emotion.

It strikes me that the way to begin is with little steps, modestly, in daily and hourly confrontation with seemingly small questions caused by a potpourri of anxieties: Shall we have fish or lamb for dinner tonight? Should I drive all the way down-island to the fish market, or should I settle for meat at the mid-island market? And does it matter, in terms of nutrition or taste, whether we have fish or meat tonight? And, as well, what is it that has priority here, in terms of convenience and ease for me? If going for meat seems kinder to me than going for fish, and fish is not nutritionally preferable tonight, then why not settle for "being kind to Peggy" (my husband's theme song) and go for meat? Why not, indeed?

It is to be hoped that eventually, when I am confronted by larger dilemmas than what to have for dinner, when I am confronted, for example, with a dilemma as large and as significant as whether or not to remind Nick that it is time for his monthly blood test (which he is deliberately ignoring), it is, yes, devoutly to be hoped that I will be better able to deal with these irresolutions because I have unceasingly been "shaping" my mind in practicing minor decision making.

In other words, try to know my own mind. And when in doubt, try to seek the answer as to why. This should be a daily, unflinching task, entered into with the belief that my mind, helped by the subliminal preparation for conscious action, will begin gradually to declare itself as shaper and controller.

And so, at last, this total mind of mine, which has all along been so "unwieldy" and so "obstinate," may begin to declare itself to me as "turning pliant," and both hemispheres of it may have found a more balanced interdependence, a more profitable coexistence, "the extraordinary union of regnant intellect with ill-starred temperament."[26]

The third step is to free the mind. It is a splendid-sounding destination—freedom—that everyone on earth wants and knows something about, either through possession of it or through lack of it. Though for innumerable people the attainability of their inalienable rights, let alone their inalienable needs, is limited by their human predicament, or even by their potential. And so freedom, to many, remains perhaps forever only a promise.

Freedom, however, is a result. Freedom is not action, it is the result of action. And because of that, I believe that it "will come of itself into your hands" as a result of the endeavors of "knowing" and "shaping."

Eventually, I believe that "knowing" and "shaping" and "freeing," like a troika, will all be going along together.

While understanding is growing, will continue to grow, will never stop growing, and while both subliminal and conscious "shaping" is proceeding hand in hand and open-endedly with it, while this applied cooperative wisdom is taking place, along with its first disclosure of some sort of freedom from crippling fears and actions, then there can be an opportunity for an expanding new experience of what freedom is like and what it can promise: that "freedom is man's progress in returning to himself."[27]

11 Taking Action

I May, I Might, I Must

If you will tell me why the fen
appears impassable, I then
will tell you why I think that I
can get across it if I try.

—Marianne Moore[28]

I HAVE a way of postponing making decisions. A package of medium-size garbage bags—the wrong size and so it must be returned for the right size—will lie on the front hall bench for two weeks, and even though each time I pass it I take note that it looks out of place on that polished-from-long-use, hand-carved wooden bench, I still can't arrive at a moment of decision that results in taking it back to the market.

Day after day the red and yellow box remains precisely there, where it can't be overlooked, presumably to facilitate its being returned. But evidently I don't want to go to the trouble of doing this picayune errand. Perhaps it stays there because I occasionally ask myself whether it is worth $2.78 to take it out to the car, put it in the backseat, then, when I get to the market, take it out of the car and in to the cashier, explain why it is being returned, and ask for a refund.

It is picayune, and I have wasted endless wattage on the yeses and nos of indecision, hours of confused and balking thought about an issue that isn't worth three minutes of indecision. (I wonder if I have unconsciously chosen garbage bags as an example of the waste of indecision?)

"Waste not, want not," was the dictate of my mother's household, run with Scottish thrift. So possibly a war for or against Scottish thrift is going on in me, as well as the basic inability to make up my mind.

Anyway, indecisiveness is always a great hang-up for me, and I love that expression, which so precisely describes what goes on in an indecisive person. I have a scene-on-a-Grecian-urn image of myself hanging by the label on the neck of my coat, my arms and legs frozen as they began their flailings, their protest against being hung up—forever there, forever flailing.

There is not always tomorrow.

As I say this to myself, at last I believe it.

With sudden impatience, I realize that I can't, like a trapeze artist, suspend myself airily from insight to insight—such as seeing the sea as separate from me, or being out of my egoistic self as I was in the Payne Whitney interviews—complacently interpreting these little miracles as the fait accompli of progress and never coming down to earth.

Another, smaller thing: I can't continue to palm off my indecisiveness and inaction on being a Pisces—those two ambivalent fish swimming in opposite directions—which I have always done with a certain amount of playfulness, but seriously too. How many Pisces persons churn themselves in all directions except forward with that swizzle stick?

I simply do not any longer want to pretend that waiting for insight or blaming inaction on a zodiacal constellation or simply procrastinating because I don't know my own mind, is a reasonable or valid excuse for stalemate. I am too old. There is not always tomorrow.

But there is, clearly and limitlessly, today.

And so, here I am at last, today, face-to-face with something I can no longer postpone and have no wish to, i.e., how to translate those months of philosophizing into activity and to metamorphose my armchair convictions of how to bring about change into a living out of them.

I am ready to graduate, and now I must go out into the world, get down to brass tacks and put to use what I have learned.

I have learned about my egoism, about the tigers and the strawberry, and about the suffering that is for fools. I have learned that seeing a world filtered by myself does not work and that I must see beyond myself if it is to work. I know which parts of myself are for all time and which parts are not. And I have learned that Margaret must now, for the third time in her life, "apply her mind," and this time lastingly.

But how can I begin to translate all this knowledge into a living out of it?

Is it possible to take action today about these basic, repetitive questions:

How, practically and strategically, can I keep alert to my egoism in an action kind of way, if such a thing is possible?

How can I attempt to take in, with an hour-to-hour attentiveness, what is going on right under my nose?

And how, specifically, can I begin to deal with fear when a sudden attack of it sets me spinning and its darkness settles over me? How, precisely, do I behave, what steps do I take mentally and emotionally, when I hear of a friend's serious illness and soon, with furtive fear, start looking at my own body for possible symptoms of the same disease?

How do I actually do it? And I mean *do it*, not just think about doing it. That stalemate has been the unfinished business of my life—the promise to myself to act and the failure to do so—an intellectual understanding of dominant drives but an inability to control the drives. "Knowing" versus "doing." For me, understanding has never been enough to turn my behavior around.

Unfortunately for the implementation of this "doing," the common approach to just that—such as consciously coming to grips with the problem facing me—has never worked for me. I don't believe I have ever solved anything by telling myself to.

That being the case, can I willfully set about an action program of change?

I have always loved the tempestuously transitional month of March because it is the certain promise of change. Bare earth *will* change to bountiful earth. My contracted and contained spirit *will* loosen and open out, along with leaves opening and frozen brooks beginning to flow.

In early spring, on the sixth of March, my birthday comes as well, always bringing the reminder that change will, in a few more weeks, begin.

And the migrating return of the red-wing blackbird to the island has been on or about the sixth of March ever since we moved here twenty-five years ago. Time after time, like a message just for me (egoism?), miraculously I have heard on that day its first jubilant *conk-er-eee, conker-er-eee.* Spring is here, it announces from the top of the big juniper by the deck. Change is on its way.

Since I have always been propelled by the promise of change, I think that without my being conscious of it, each red-wing song, and each birthday, is just another stimulus toward the hope and the promise of change.

This birthday Nick gave me hearts:

A small, heart-shaped braided rug in softly blended light and dark blue calicoes, for the blue guest room.

Three heart-shaped straw baskets—small, medium, large—that fit within one another, to be used for cut-up French bread in a folded napkin or for a small box of spring pansies, or whatever.

Six kitchen towels, three red, three blue, with a pattern of hearts.

A thing you press down hard onto red paper, which cuts out and ejects little tiny hearts. I will fill the envelopes of letters to my grandchildren with handfuls of them, so that when the letters are opened, a small avalanche of hearts will spill out.

And a long, charm-bracelet type of necklace, with all kinds and sizes of hearts dangling from it.

Fear seems far away as I lift that lovely necklace over my head and look down at the gold outline of a heart embedded with small pearls.

* * *

Change.

Some people never give up hoping for it, and can change. They work honestly for it, their integrity dictating.

But some play games with hope for it, and do not change. Often they are the ones whose hopes lend themselves to the postponing devices of resolution makers. Like me. Resolutions can be rules and, as they were for me, authoritative. And though I believe that resolve is a basic begetter of reform, I realize that when resolve begins to bog down in insincere resolution or borrows the language of totalitarian rules, its nature changes.

I was subjected to a religious, conformist, steel-strict kind of upbringing, a virtual legal system of behavior laws. I was taught to believe that rules rule, that "do" rules make for happiness and success and and that "don't" rules make for unhappiness and failure, and I was punished if I disobeyed them. I was given images of perfection such as the Ten Commandments but was not, at the same time, given the kind of flexible interpretation of them that could develop my capacity truly to believe in them and to try to fulfill their images. Nor was I given the kind of tutelage or example that would help me develop my own goals, my own image of a happy self.

When I was a striving child, I kept by my bed a little book my parents had put there called *Daily Thoughts for Daily Needs*. On its title page was a verse by Thomas Carlyle: "So here has been dawning another blue day. Think, wilt thou let it slip useless away?"[29]

Every morning I opened this book and first read the exhortatory verse by Carlyle, then turned to the thought for the day—someone else's inspirational poetry or prose, intended to spark my awakening with hope and purpose. Every morning of my teens, I depended on someone else's rule for growth and fulfillment and never thought to consult myself as to whether I had any better ideas. Day after day I made a resolution to be useful or to be patient or to love my neighbor as myself or to control my temper, while dreamily postponing enactment until the more possible future. There was always tomorrow.

Rules, rules. All my life I have been trying to resist misguided discipline—my parents' and my own, for surely I internalized that stern stuff. The part of me that knows better has in the long run never been able to stomach that kind of reform. Telling myself to do something always feels like a discipline to be distrusted and resisted—the whip that was always there, not only in the hands of parental survey but also in my own unwitting hands.

I can still hear Father, his mouth a strict line beneath melancholy, uncertain eyes, saying sternly, "Your finger bowl is not to drink from, Margaret," when, in a rare instance of prankish rebellion, I had picked it up to drink from it. He had kept a manners score sheet on the dining room table, next to his plate, and on it marked down all of Wint's and my wrongs for future reckoning and all of our rights for future reward. He had score sheets for everything: for the condition of my bureau drawers, for the way Wint and I behaved in church. For mischievousness, disobedience and unruliness, he kept in the back of his clothes closet, behind his row of boots, a short-handled, coiled, stinging serpent of a whip with which in displaced fury he "thrashed" (his word) our soft little white bottoms and the backs of our short legs, leaving red welts.

I became a person who rebelliously did not want to be told what to do. And now, so many years after I first began to be subjected to, and to subject myself to, the thou shalts and thou shalt nots, I still do not want to go about this new adventure of learning by holding that kind of whip over my head.

I think that this is why the idea of "letting go" has always appealed to me so much. "That which is for you will come of itself into your hands, but if you strive to overtake it, you will destroy that lovely flower of your peace that is so short of blooming."

When I first heard those words from *The Dance of Shiva*—initially enticing and persuasive because of the legitimacy of being ancient wisdom, and then exciting because they felt like the antithesis of discipline—I seized them, I clung to them. Here was a whole, lovely notion of giving sensibility more respectability than sense and of denying the value of sense in favor of sensibility.

This was a new, liftoff kind of idea for me, one that promised a freedom from that "discipline" that I had always sensed was not from the heart but from the head. Here was ancient philosophic wisdom assuring me that prosaic thinking was the very opposite of poetic, undisciplined being and was not the way for a puritan to go.

And so, with the pleasant, easy feeling that I could reliably sink back into those words and be reassured by them, I said to myself reverently and with immense relief, "Let that be the way."

And actually, even midway through this thinking/writing project, I was still comforting myself by saying, "Good, I should stop working at trying to improve. I should sit back and let things happen to me, instead of trying to make things happen." I would remind myself that I am a puritan and that those words from *The Dance of Shiva* were a warning to me to give up a puritanical pursuit of betterment. I love the expression "laid back," and that's what I wanted to be.

However, recently it began to enter my head that I could use *it*, rather than just emotions. I began to grasp the possibilities of using sense instead of sensibility. The Payne Whitney interviews had shown me the good uses I could put my mind to if I wanted to. (Why do I keep forgetting this?) And I am now beginning to think about "thinking," about how little of it I have done and how much of it I could do, day by day, if only I knew how to get going without the goad and the stimulation of something like a Payne Whitney interview.

I do believe that I am beginning at last to grasp the fact that such a laissez-faire attitude as being exclusively laid back can make the gestating gestalt deficient in one important element—the input of practiced "thinking"—and have begun to question the denial of conscious endeavor advocated by those *Dance of Shiva* words.

Carl Jung says, "Experience has taught me that some familiarity with the psychology of dreams will often lead people to an exaggerated trust in the unconscious, which impairs the conscious power of decision. The unconscious functions satisfactorily only when consciousness fulfills the task to the limits of its capacity."

I do realize that it has been a helpless feeling to float along on the ups and downs of a subliminal stream in which I seem to have no conscious control, waiting for the occasional enlightened moment; or to wake in the morning to an unexpectedly delightful frame of mind and to have no idea what brought it about, unless it was sweet dreams.

And so, in the last few months, I have begun to hear

those *Dance of Shiva* words differently: not with the desirous interpretation I once gave them, but with a different interpretation entirely. I see them as preaching against the wrong kind of effort—in my case, that lifelong anxiety-propelled striving for what I don't in truth need but seem to think I need—the perfect life lived by the perfect person and all the accoutrements that fortify that sort of superstar. I see those words now as being simply a warning about the rigidities and misguidedness of egoism, rather than as a mindless reliance on emotional and instinctual being. In my own words, "What is best for me will come for me out of my own self, and not from an egotistical kind of striving."

I am trying to formulate a way of advancing that does not view "discipline" as a totalitarian menace, as the kind of authoritative unpleasantness I have been trying all my life to resist.

And much as I wince at the word "discipline," I now see that in the self-mastery I am obviously aiming for, there will have to be some discipline. Not the laying-on-thick kind of arbitrary Ten Commandment-isms I grew up with, but rather a discipline that knowledgeably and encouragingly tells me "I can" and "I will."

And possibly what is begging to be in operation here, instead of a horrid disciplinary tactic, is a developing conceivability that is the product of that gestating gestalt—an awakening, you might say—a growing, enlarging employment of the sense side of the brain along with a tempering of the ongoing lavish productivity of the sensibility side. There are two engines up there, the right one working overtime, the left one working far below its capacity. My wish is to try to equalize their workings, "that mind and soul, according well, may make one music."[30]

In other words, I've got to pay more attention to a new concept of discipline—the respectful kind. At last such discipline has an authority I *do* respect. It even has a practicality and a logic.

And so, instead of hugging to myself those *Dance of Shiva* words, which, given one interpretation, could encourage me to give up what I see as discipline and just "let go," I must remember that conscious effort will "sink in," to use another appropriate cliché. Reliance on the gestating gestalt does not need to exclude a deliberate use of the mind. The practice of conscious thinking will filter down and be assimilated into the unconscious and, yeasting there, will be developmental at that level, becoming an enlarging, fertile element of it.

On the subject of taking action or when to take action or even what to take action about, here is a tale I wrote down in my journal when it happened last week, hoping that by writing it I could resolve my dilemma about it.

> April 3. A.M. After only four hours of sleep: Should I or should I not keep on maneuvering to kiss Nick good night? It's almost a week now, and it looks as though it's not going to work out.
>
> Should I stop? But I love to kiss him. I love the taste of his mouth. I always have. It is a sweet taste, now as then, not to mention that it is, now as then, a beautiful mouth to look at, always expressive to me of Nick's inner beauty, which is, of course, one of the reasons I love to kiss him.

Months, years had gone by since we had kissed each other's mouths as a regular thing, and then, suddenly one morning, the goodness of kissing was revived.

It was last Friday, the day I went to Boston to have my yearly checkup with the gynecologist. I was in the front hall, about to leave for the boat, coat on, bag slung over shoulder, hand on doorknob. Nick was there, standing tentatively in the long hall doorway with the courteous patience a person has when he's dutifully seeing someone off and hopes to get the little ceremony over with soon so that he can get back to what he was doing. Or so it seemed to me. Or was he standing there to wave good-bye, so to speak, out of duty, or courtesy? Or from long habit? Or because it is what a man does when his wife is about to embark on a journey to Boston to see her doctor? Or from a heartfelt desire to wish his wife well on her visit to a doctor and to let her know that he's with her?

Whichever it was, it was mostly, I think, an unusual attentiveness to me, for suddenly he made an abrupt, spontaneous movement toward me, thrust his head out and kissed me on the mouth—a full, sweet, short-lasting but plentiful kiss. If only he could have known what support for the dreaded doctor's visit that was. More support than any words could possibly have been.

And then again, that evening, miracle of miracles, when I returned home in the dark of the windy night and came into the warmth and light of the front hall—bone tired I was—"Darling," came his voice from the living room where the fire crackled, "you're back!" And then there he was in the hall, coming swiftly to kiss me. On the mouth. Eagerly, truly, he put his smiling mouth on mine. Oh, after this long day, here it was again! This, and the relief of having had a good report from the doctor, made the moment so full and potent and perfect.

As I lay in bed that night waiting for sleep and thinking about the strange miracle wrought by kissing, I made up my mind to take action about it. After all, I was in the midst of writing about taking action. Suit action to the word, I said to myself. Reinstate kissing good night, as a regular thing.

Clearly I would have to be the one to start it and to keep it up. Because I know that, aside from the eloquent ceremony of those kisses of my going and returning, Nick would not think, in an everyday way, to kiss me good night. Ever. That is, unless he was moved to do so spontaneously. (Which I suppose, I admit, I concede, is after all the heart of the matter.)

The next night, after dinner, sitting by a dying fire that was now only two graying logs on andirons above a live gold eye of an ember glowing beneath them that, though fire, could not now, in its separation from the cooling logs above it, possibly ignite them (how ironically symbolic)—sitting there getting ready to get up and gather my glasses and my book and my sweater and my courage, I thought, now I will go over and kiss him.

He was lying back on the loveseat, his head on a cushion, his eyes closed.

Unsurely, I went over, I leaned down. I put a kiss on his mouth.

His eyes flew open and widened with surprise and pleasure.

I was so relieved, I was suddenly, again, so happy. It could be done. Like the single ember, I glowed.

Resolution to keep on doing this was now bedrock and stimulating and strong with promise. So the next night I set myself in the mode, when bedtime came, to continue the kissing.

However, Nick had gotten up from the fireside to go to bed before I was ready to leave it and the last chapter of my book. And when I did get up and go into my bedroom, he had already disappeared into his bathroom and shut the door.

I undressed. I did my teeth. I turned down my bed. I filled my hot water bottle and put it between the sheets. I then sat down on the edge of the bed and waited. I sat in the coolness of the room that was not the warmth of the inviting bed I wanted to be in and waited for him to come out of the bathroom. There I sat, uncomfortably chilly. Waiting. Lying in wait. The thought crossed my mind that this was mildly ridiculous.

Finally, hell's bells, I thought, I'm getting into bed. But just as I was about to, his bathroom door opened and out he came, heading for his bedroom.

I leaped up. I went through the door that joins our rooms and stood self-consciously (really not liking this by now) while he turned down his bed and got into it. Then, feeling very foolish and very nervous, I went over to him and thrust my head down to him and touched a kiss to his surprised mouth.

He smiled, nervously.

That was all.

Deflated, feeling absurd and humiliated, I turned away without comment and went back to my bed.

Yet for two more nights I "accosted" him. Yes, that was the way it was beginning to feel to me, like a Peter Sellers bedroom farce. I would lie in wait, sitting on the edge of my bed, until he was appropriately available. Then I would go in and kiss him. His little embarrassed sound of surprise was unvarying.

The fourth night I said to hell with this and went to bed as I usually did, reading until Nick would come out of his bathroom and then, ritualistically, come to the door joining our rooms to say good night and then to close it. But I was harboring the thought, the hope, that he would have decided, before saying good night, to turn the tables and to come over and kiss me.

He came to the door, as usual. He said good night, as usual. He smiled, as usual.

I said good night. I smiled. There seemed to be a second's hesitation, a moment loud with an emptiness needing to be filled with something from one of us or from both of us.

But, unfilled, the moment ended, and Nick closed the door.

Symbolic, the closing of the door.

I sat there, thinking, wondering. Could it be that possibly he had forgotten, the day after the first mutually desired good-night kiss, all about kissing? Or even, had he sensed my "project" for reinstating kissing and, being nondevious Nick, felt that mine was a contrived performance and fundamentally rejected it as such? Or was it, I wondered, that the diminution in him, actually the absence in him now, of desire made him uneasy in the presence of the strength of mine? Where was ardor in him? Or rather, was it in him at all? For the space of one day he had wanted to kiss me. A brief revival of ardor? Or the memory of lost ardor? Or what?

Settle for it, I told myself. Let kissing be mutual or not at all. Stop trying to force kissing that doesn't come naturally. As long as love remains, ardor can be parted with.

It was worth a try, though.

Nick's eightieth birthday on board Daughter of Dove

12 Paying Attention

I BEGAN the last chapter with the question: Can I willfully set about an action program for change? And I am cautiously beginning to believe that, if I put my mind to it, I can.

Back to that question. Can I, knowing that I am self-concerned and inattentive, do anything to become less so (for I know that I cannot be self-concerned and at the same time attentive)? Can I, willfully, mindfully, set about an action program of shaping that will begin to dissipate concentration on myself? Is there a way to literally "put my mind to it," to attempt to take in, with an hour-to-hour concentration, what I am seeing and being?

In other words, are there specific, everyday actions I can take to encourage less self-concern and more attentiveness? Without the challenge of a Payne Whitney interview, how can I begin, today, to concentrate on me looking rather than on me?

Do I, for instance, wake up in the morning and say to myself, "Today I am going to put into practice what I have all along been talking about. I am going to start paying attention. I am having lunch today with Diana, and I am going to make a point of taking her in. I am going to remind myself, force myself, to pay close attention to her throughout the meal, to stop appraising her, to stop assessing my feelings about her, to *think* about her, not about myself. I am going to let her be there more than I am there, let her be what she is, separate from my assessment of her, as I was separate from the sea that day on the beach long ago. I am going to let her be her fact, not my fiction." I remembered that statement of Philip O'Connor's about "the art of ceasing to live a drama in order to see one."[31]

I tell myself that this is what I must do. But doesn't it feel artificial and arbitrary? Can I sincerely and effectively do this? Won't my attention falter and stray, so that in no time I'll be back in the old self-focused groove of not really absorbing what Diana is saying because I'm too busy planning what I'll say to her when she has stopped talking, or too busy trying to take her in, forcing myself to take her in, to really take her in?

It feels unnatural and unworkable, too, to imagine myself looking out the window and devoting my mind and emotions to the beauty of the snow-covered field and the crows flying while at the same time trying to *force* myself to take in that presence and that reality unfiltered by my misleading sensibilities. And I'm even certain that it wouldn't work perfectly, as it once did, to look at the sea and simultaneously to recognize that it was separate from me. Because "it is common experience that nothing ruins 'a pleasure' so much as watching yourself in the midst of it to see whether it pleases you. You can only live in one moment at a time, and you cannot think simultaneously about listening to the waves and whether you are enjoying listening to the waves."[32]

And so I wonder whether expectations of having my cake and eating it too are unrealizable because it is simply not possible consciously, in one instant, to banish everything that for a lifetime has gotten in the way of a kind of seeing that loses me in the seeing. I will see, optically, what I am looking at, and perhaps this time with more vitality and attention and without the old dread of knowing I won't always be here to see it, but will I absorb it in its perfect separateness from me, which is true, full-dimensional perception?

And so does it mean that the conscious effort to look at and to take in what I am looking at freezes me rather than expands me and thus fails in the endeavor, and that therefore the endeavor should not be made? Does it mean that deliberately setting out to view the world beyond myself is useless, or that consciously striving to stop, to look, to listen proves always to be one-dimensional?

No. It does not. I feel this, all of a sudden, decidedly, and my doubts begin to vanish. I see that in the deliberate disciplinary practice of attempting to pay attention to what I am viewing, I *suspend judgment* about it as I did in the Payne Whitney interviews, I will, at least for a moment, stop having points of view not pertaining to it, which may, in turn, give me a chance to see it unclothed of *me*. And at the same time I will, I do believe, be unconsciously penetrating the attitudes I have always had of looking but not seeing, and beginning to break them up. For a second, I will have experienced the novelty of seeing and being in a world unfiltered by me—an experience that will not be forgotten.

And so I return to my positive-minded belief that there can be additional and different action for tackling (shaping) self-concern and attentiveness, along with the long-term, self-analytical kind. "To know the mind" is, of course, an essential foundation for understanding self-concern and for trying to recover from it, for, as I said earlier, self-concern is what I innately *am not*, and so I must first find out what I innately *am*, in order to proceed successfully.

But further, I must continuously remember the Payne Whitney interviews and the attentiveness that enabled me to step out of my egoistic self and into the person I was interviewing—an all-inclusive regardful experience of looking at someone and knowing him for what he is, not as someone changed by me into what he is not.

Yes. I must continuously remember that my self-located looking is what I innately am not. And thus a world seen and interpreted through that kind of looking is something it is not. In doing this, I narrow my recognition of everything, giving myself, through this distorted view, an unreal sense of both myself and the world I live in. In viewing myself unreally, I accustom myself to viewing everything unreally (including the prospect of my own extinction). For any full-fledged egoist, what an unimaginable horror the thought of his own extinction must be! "How can such a thing happen to me?" he cries, and gets no answer.

Basically I must encourage in myself, when I am with others, the attentiveness to the present moment that all along has been trying to have some kind of life. I must try to use in each circumstance as much persuasive intellectual persistence as I am capable of, making a concentrated effort to suspend the habit of relying on critical, personal, even conventional associative ideas and images about what I am looking at, which, because of the overlay of me on it, will cause it to seem what it essentially is not.

Thus, with discipline, the sense side of my mind could become habituated to the effort to view the reality of what I am looking at—the fog, the sea separate from me, my friend Diana at lunch—and, cooperatively with the sensibility side and with all the other forces that join in processing and establishing experience in the gestating gestalt, could gradually facilitate an ability to be in and to perceive more fully and less subjectively the contents of my world.

I even begin to hope, or actually to believe, that one day I will be sitting with my friend Diana at lunch and suddenly, with no conscious effort on my part, a fuller comprehension of her will be there, will have come of itself into my hands.

Eventually (who knows), through all the processes in me—including the incomprehensible maneuverings of the gestating gestalt—that are at work to understand and to tackle my self-concern, perhaps the necessity of policing it will fade a bit, as to a limited extent self-concern itself may. Obviously, I will never be wholly free of it. I don't think anyone ever is, except here and there a saint. But if—in action, and in thoughts—my self-concern at last begins to be less dominating, I may then to some extent stop dwelling so much on the word "egoism" and experience only the *deed*. A new freedom?

My friend Penny sent me a postcard from her father's sixty-fifth college reunion. He had asked her to go with him, and she went.

On the card, Penny told me that she had met an eighty-seven-year-old man, a retired headmaster of a boys' boarding school, who charmed her (Penny is fifty-seven). In a conversation evidently interesting to both of them, he told her that, at his age, he was just beginning to grow up.

Isn't egoism essentially childlike? And would it be wise to say that what we really have to do in order to outgrow it is simply to grow up?

* * *

But stop here. Uneasily I realize that there are questions about being in the present moment that I haven't been paying attention to and should.

First: If I did manage, without the stage set of a Payne Whitney interview, to achieve the experience of being in the present moment, would I know it? Would I actually be feeling something that told me, "Oh yes, good, this is what it is to be in the present moment, and it feels wonderful"?

Well, of course, no. This is not what happened in the interviews. I knew afterward that I had been liberated in a new, fountainlike way. But during the interviews I wasn't at all saying to myself that I was having an unusual experience. I may have been sensing a certain ease at having ceased to feel besieged by profuse and self-destructive thoughts, but I wasn't declaring this ease to myself as the state of being in the present moment, since I was in that state *because* I had managed to suspend judgment about what I was seeing and thinking, and thus no self-conscious thoughts were present at all. The experience of the interviews wasn't so much what I was feeling as what I was not feeling.

And so I will say again: The ultimate is to experience without being aware of anything but experience.

And another question: We are born with the need to think about the future, if only about where the next meal is coming from. Hope is a part of this—hope of getting well if we are sick, of growing up if we are little, of a child coming, of spring coming, of love coming. It is innate, and for many reasons—survival among them—essential for any living thing to be concerned with the future, to look forward.

Why, then, am I so intent on the need not to be concerned with the future? Am I trying to do away with something instinctual that hasn't a chance of being done away with?

Oh, I don't think so at all. It seems to me evident that if my need to look forward becomes unnatural, or obsessional or fantasy-prone, then it has gone beyond bounds and should be seen as abnormal.

Or even if my need to look forward is a so-called normal occupation with becoming, I will, I hope, become more to my own liking if, through paying attention to "now" rather than "then," I give myself a chance to see the world as it is and me as I truly am in it.

So. A moderate occupation with what is going to happen to me and how or whether I can control it is normal. But a preoccupation with fears of the future, an incessant dwelling on this, is abnormal and will prevent me from living freely, where life will be real, in the deepest and best sense of realness. That will be a life situation I can deal with, not a life situation that deals with me.

I may have suggested that being in the present moment is a rarefied and particularized experience. Not so. The blessings of it are quite naturally and even ordinarily experienced by thousands and thousands everywhere. Visual artists—painters, sculptors, photographers—are enviable to me because they have to be constantly focusing on what they are looking at. And not only artists; anyone whose vocation or avocation demands, for success, a ready and focused and nonsubjective attention, is living to a great extent in the present moment. When your mind doesn't wander self-destructively from the task at hand that is absorbing most of your attention—playing the flute, turning the heel of a sock—you are very much in the present moment.

This means that most of us are in the present moment far more than we realize. Even though a certain amount of random thinking is always going on and is inevitable, it doesn't prevent a certain amount, also, of fruitful (strawberry) awareness of all that the mind and senses are constantly taking in.

Third and last: How can I go about attempting to cast out fear? Is there an immediate, conscious process of trying to halt and do away with fear, be it chronic fear or a fresh onslaught of it?

I have an answer. Perhaps it is best given by recounting what happened to me or, I should say, what I caused to happen to me in three successive phases, in three different ways.

The first phase was a short period of being without fear—not through a conscious process of trying to deal with the fear, but through a sudden, unwilled action.

I had been in a long phase of feeling slightly smothered with a faint and nameless dread—not a real depression, I don't have those, but some still thing sensed mostly as an absence of joy (like the peaches in the market suddenly not being peaches as I knew them). I was conscious of being tired of it. I tried to write it out. Much came from the pencil onto the pad, but no sudden insight, no evident relief.

Then one day, I was standing by my bedpost, looking out the window. Suddenly I felt within me a departure, as though something had simply left my body, opened a door and gone out of it. I was then wonderfully empty. No dread.

What a miraculous riddance! It gave me such lightness. Yet I had no understanding of how or why it had happened, only a rooted and elated feeling of such action being possible. The way a growing flower might feel if it had emotions?

All I could tell myself was that it had simply gone away; no more than that. At the moment, I didn't really care about what had caused it. All I cared about was that it felt perfectly wonderful to be normal again.

The second phase was a process that I believe was partly conscious and partly subconscious, a fledgling but earnest will to put my mind to it, backed up, needless to say, by the subterranean simmerings of the gestating gestalt.

One day, or during a period of days, I came into another blessed state of being without the sensation of fear. But this time, I was without it because each time it occurred to me to look for it, I steered clear of it. In other words, I kept saying to myself, "Where is fear?" but never once allowed myself to feel it.

I remained in this carefree state for weeks, feeling proud of my power. It was as though I stood clear of the fear, but implicit in this was the knowledge of its being off there somewhere, waiting to spring. Nevertheless, I kept it at bay simply by not permitting it to enter me. Of course, it wasn't a wholly carefree feeling, because I was constantly aware of the effort to keep it in its place.

In a confidently and calmly embattled way, I was on the defensive, and yet I felt powerful because I was in control, I was in the known process of "shaping" and was not permitting the invasion.

Then one day, fear was back again, and my power was gone. Why this worked as it did, or whether it was a dependable process that could be repeated, I didn't know. But I was certain that something had worked, and I had become, as a result, subtly reinforced and cautiously confident.

The third phase was an action that was wholly conscious, though of course backed up by all the rest of my inner workings.

One stormy April day, I went to visit an acquaintance in a nursing home over on the Cape. Returning from it, I was in a sort of generalized state of horror. The shock of such a place is I'm sure known to everyone, but it was only the second time in my life that I had been exposed to one like this, and it was a deeply disturbing experience. In an antiseptic, arid, regimented sense it was squalor—squalor of place and persons. It was helplessness, joylessness, hopelessness and finality.

When I got home I burst into the house and cried out to Nick, "Never, never, no matter what happens to us, never let's permit either one of us to go into a nursing home!"

Shortly after this outburst, I began to realize how unrealistic my reaction had been. And for an hour or so, I vacillated between the knowledge that statistically the chances of my needing a nursing home at my age were good and that it was reasonable to think it could happen to me, versus the awareness that there was no certainty it would happen to me and that I was again wallowing in the kind of pessimistic prophesying that had become my habit and my self-identity at this age.

I was keenly alert to what was going on, I suppose because these alarms had become increasingly and inescapably obvious. And so, shortly, alert to the need to take myself in hand and to the absolute necessity of not permitting myself to backslide—a sort of now-or-never feeling—I floundered badly for a moment, old habit wrestling with new thought, and then, in a moment, I settled for thought.

I mean to say that I deliberately favored my mind. I made myself think. I "shaped."

I did not start to think from the angle of present reality, which was that I was perfectly free of symptoms of illness, I was happy in the here and now, I was free at the moment from dramatic emotional burden, I was in my own sun-filled home, not in a nursing home. I did not start from that angle, because at the moment it was not as real to me as my vivid worries. I've learned from experience that it is most effective first to dispel the darkness of fantasies in order to enter into the all-clear of a freed mind.

And so I started to think from the angle of my imagined fate. I began with the fantasies. I inspected all of them, the nursing home I could be in, the illnesses I could have and so forth.

I then began my litany for exorcising the devil. I searched for the first word of it: reality. I got it, slippery, elusive. I managed to hold on to it.

Reality, I repeated to myself, the reality of this minute is that there is not one single thing about my physical state that even remotely suggests I should go into a nursing home. However, the reality of the next minute after this one, of the next hour, the next day, the next month, even the next year, is its unknownness: I may, or then again, I may not, have to go into a nursing home.

That unknownness is a certainty, an absolutely undeniable, certifiable fact, I told myself and knew it. Therefore, if I want to feel safe in this moment, what I have to do is to stay with the certainty of right now, stay in this only sure moment.

This litany did not work immediately, and release from the worry did not come right away. But I kept after it. And finally, later that afternoon, as I was walking up the road to the mailbox, suddenly the whole "foolish" enterprise I was engaged in became clear, and I saw and knew my imagined fears for what they were—self-serving flights of fantasy and actually, in terms of the reality of me in this moment as well as in terms of a serious lapse of my intelligence, lunacy.

I saw the whole performance as not only crazy but a bore. I decided to stop the process right then, that minute.

And it did stop. It simply went away. I felt, triumphantly, that it could stop. I mean that *I* could stop it. Not conclusively, I knew. But for the moment, instead of a racket in me, there was an emptiness, giving space.

I had taken action.

It was within my power to take action.

It could be done, and I had done it. I had "shaped."

Comfortably, but still precariously, I was experiencing the word "freedom."

So what does all this signify about an action program for change?

What it signifies, I think, is that I have come to a point in myself, through one means and another, of readiness to act. Or, as I said before, I am ready to graduate. And it signifies that underneath the gradual and powerfully apprehended necessity to become attentive—to my egoism, to my fears, to people, to the world of nature, actually to all of life—I have already begun a kind of action, the paramount action from which attentiveness and all other action derives. I mean that I have begun to "shape my mind."

I am realizing that a goal I have long since begun to strive for without knowing it, or naming it as paramount and as underlying everything else, is a fuller reliance on the deliberate use of the mind.

I believe that during the writing of this book, the gestating gestalt—that reliable and sublime process of both subterranean and conscious forces—has been receiving, along with everything else, a steady input of new concepts about the importance of disciplined thinking, and that an unprecedented but ongoing *mental* activity has at last begun to declare itself. So much so that finally, like the sun coming out from the clouds, there, visible, stands the mind—the light by which, from now on, my life in its entirety must be seen.

And so, as well as urging myself to take new action, I must understand that action has all along been taken, and to the extent that I have at last given the full use of the mind not only its due but its go-ahead signal.

Here, to end this chapter, is a love story about taking action.

On a cool night in late April, I prepared to turn out the light and, I hoped, go to sleep. I was depressed. And I knew the reasons why.

First, because Nick seemed more and more so frail, and I felt the physiotherapist was driving him beyond his strength, but didn't dare say so. And too, because spring, which could have lifted my spirits, was so late in coming.

And also because of having come to a sudden impasse on this book about old age—"the book," we all call it. I had almost decided to put it aside for a while and start again on the revision of my unfinished novel, which needs extensive work. Even, I thought I might abandon "the book" altogether.

Feeling dubious about the possibility of sleep in this mood, I turned out the light, felt with my feet for the hot water bottle I always put in the bed to warm it and, sighing, asked for sleep.

It did not come. And as I lay there knowing it would not, I began to think about what Nick had said to me before dinner, by the fire, as we had sat there talking about my dilemma about "the book."

"It has occurred to me," he said, "that when I get up during the night, if you're awake and would like to talk, I'll come into your room and talk with you. It might be of help, who knows. I can easily go back to sleep. That's no problem. I always go back to sleep. Think about it," he urged. "I'd like to help if I could."

Immediately I had loved the idea, and told him so.

Remembering this as I lay sleepless, I found myself almost wishing (well, no, not really) that I would be awake when I heard him going into the bathroom, as he always does once or twice during the night.

And I was. At one-thirty—I had turned on my light and looked at my watch when I heard him going into the bathroom—I called out to him as I heard him come out of it. Eagerly, even like a longing child in the dark of the night, I called out to him, "Nick, I'm awake. You said you'd talk to me. Please, will you?"

He came right away into my room. He got a blanket and settled in my big chair. And I began to talk. "I've started to rethink the middle section of the novel," I said, "the one that needs the work. And, yes, I can see what perhaps could be done. I suppose I can do it. But my heart isn't in it! I can't generate any longing or need to be back in that novel!"

Nick sat for a long time without answering. He does that. Sometimes you wonder if he is going to answer at all. Finally, he said, "What you should ask yourself is, what do you *want* to do?"

I, too, thought for a minute, encouraged toward a clear answer to a clear question. Then I said, "The only thing I'm really thinking about, day and night, is 'the book.'"

The next morning I woke up (obviously you wake up only if you've slept) to a sunny day. It was even a fairly warm day—in the fifties. I sensed that my shadowy mood had been eclipsed by a brighter one. A flood of positivism poured into me. The conviction that work on "the book" was of necessity ended had been replaced not only by an openness toward it but by the restoration of the old familiar belief in it that had not once failed me in all the months of working on it.

I saw then what had discouraged me about it—a sudden move toward intellectualism, searching Erik Erikson's writings for his definition of self-identity, having bogged down temporarily in my own definition of it. It seemed that the more I read that great thinker, the more I found out how much I did not know about human development. Finally, my mind had spun, split and then closed up.

But this morning, "the book," instead of being an abandoned manuscript shut away in a file drawer, was once again a tenable work in progress lying with a promising potential on the table by my writing chair, as it had for ten months. What had felt impossible last night was familiarly possible this morning. Confusion and defeat had been swept away, and my mind was now cleared for sensible purpose.

Thanks to Nick and his on-target, clarifying question, like a light turned on in a dark room. Perhaps if someone else had asked me that question, or even if I had asked myself the question, the same mental clearance and liberation would not have resulted.

But it was not someone else. It was Nick.

Was that all I needed? "Call me but love, and I'll be new baptized."[33]

13 Endings and Beginnings

NICK IS DEAD. I write this. I have made myself write this. In facing the putting of this down on paper, I have forced myself to try to make it real. But it is not in any way real. It is only three words having nothing to do with me, appearing from my pencil onto paper. The pencil is pushed up and down automatically by fingers that are responding automatically to some staggering event that appears to have happened. The three words that have not even begun to be processed by me or to be absorbed by me have come from the top of my head to the pencil to the paper. They are not, in any way that I am conscious of, to be believed.

He died three weeks ago of a massive stroke.

That is only a statistic. That is only a statement on record on a hospital chart and in the bookkeeping of a mortuary. It has nothing to do with these summer rooms, through which the rose-sweet breeze moves, with Nick's gray Irish cardigan slung over the back of his swivel chair. It has nothing to do with his corner of the loveseat, where he sat, evenings, with his large hands crossed resignedly on his knees, his eyes far off and strong and bleak. It has nothing to do with me, because he still, vividly, alively sits there.

I have known, from the minute I was told he had died, that I was divided right down the middle by my longing, for *my* sake, to have him sitting in his corner of the loveseat across from me, and, conversely, by the clear, true violence of my not wanting him, for *his* sake, to be sitting there.

So, on some level, I am believing that he is gone, since the passionate knowledge that he is not sitting there suffering, the relief of it, the easing of the pain in my heart that his quiet suffering always caused me, makes me know that he *is* gone, from the corner of the loveseat, from the swivel chair, from his study, from his bed, from the dining room, from everywhere in what had come to be his only world—this house, this home of his.

For me, that empty chair is an emptiness vast and unknowable and unreal, as though nothing in me would ever want it to be or accept it as empty, for my missing of him sitting there makes him, indeed, powerfully there. He is everywhere in the house. Not in a ghostly sense. Not even in images of his presence. But in the way the walls, the pictures, the plants, the phone ringing, the sun on the white carpet, the screen door sticking, his slippers by his bed are just the same, just the same. The feeling of him, of us together, is just the same. The house is still lived in by us two, still for us together, as we have been in it for all these years. There is nothing that he has done or said, or that we have done or said together, that is not still vibrating in these sun-filled rooms. That empty chair is not empty of him, it is only empty of him suffering there.

* * *

Ten months have gone by since Nick's death. It is May. Beach plum is in blossom, as dazzling as Technicolor. All of nature has this scintillating vividness, a cruel, sharp beauty, not penetrating to my heart at all. Seen but not felt, as though seeing were altered and had another intention.

Nick died on the fourteenth of July. There was then no symbolism, even for me who look for symbolism, about the date of his death being the same as the date of the storming of the Bastille, the beginning of the French Revolution, but now I might say that it signified what a revolution is, "a . . . radical change."[34]

That is what it was.

And now it is time to write about it, in the context of this book. It is, I see, the fateful conclusion of my exploration of the fears of old age.

My reason for going into the detailed and very personal experience of becoming a woman who has lost a man (which in truth I have no heart for making public) is that it has so basically to do with growing up in old age, and therefore is a necessary continuation of the purpose of this book. I am writing about it, of course, primarily to help myself grasp my predicament in order to try to live with it. And, too, because I have found that my experience of widowhood is amazingly, predictably similar to the experience of other widows, that I am in a universal place thronged by millions of widows past and present. In this great fact of life, there is solace to be found, I think, in knowing that other women have endured it and have survived.

Should I have feared it? Oh yes, indeed I should have feared it! Any woman should fear it.

But although I feared what it would do to my life, I have survived what it has done to my life. And I now see that the fear of not being able to survive it was an unreal fear.

In that sense, what I will be writing about now, I hope, will show that my loss of my husband was not my end.

I was not able to take up work on the book until three months ago. At that time I came back to it, reread it, and assessed it from the point of view of all that had happened to me since the day of the beginning of radical change.

What I found out about that, and about the slow, month-by-month change that preceded it in the work on the book, I write about now, setting out, first, to summarize what the significance of the book has been to me—the sudden and astonished victim of one of those very fears of old age I had been imagining—and second, to determine whether I believe that the book can have significance for others.

I started by asking myself this question:

Has the book worked for me?

The reader, as well as I, will want to know.

The answer is: Yes, the book has worked for me.

I learned, you could say, the hard way about a certain intactness I had. Death taught me. In a way that nothing else is a substitute for, experience, quite literally, brought me to my senses. It was an immense and a staggering thing. Just that. And also unknowable. Nothing in my life has ever had this magnitude or impact.

But from it, as well as from some grown-up-ness that I believe developed through the writing of this book, I learned that I could *survive* one of the classic tragedies of old age. Contrary to all the fears I had had that if Nick died I would be so lost—no compass, no nothing—that I would fall apart completely and lastingly, I did not—at least not lastingly. At first, even though stunned, I talked, I walked, I ate (sketchily), I drank (less sketchily), I slept (usually with pills), I could smile (sometimes). In other words, to all appearances, I got by. Also, I may have been reassured by the way I was outwardly "coping"—an encouraging outer model for inner lack of it.

I have survived it. Shriveled to brown by the winter of my sorrow, I did, in the spring, come up again and put out small green shoots.

And insofar as I am able objectively to judge, I believe that the groundwork of this book was a real factor in my being able to survive it.

The consequences of being left alone were hard.

One consequence, and second only to grief, was being precipitated with horrible abruptness into the sole management, hitherto shared by two, of everything that had to do with material existence. It was, and still is, a job much too time-consuming, and demanding of skills that I do not have, to be anything but confusing and tiring in the most shattering way. This is a common occurrence in the lives of widows, I have learned. And I have also found out that, like me, women who have lost their husbands, and who immediately have to have their heads full of doctors, lawyers, merchants, chiefs, find that they have little time to think about the man whose death this is all about, no time to be where they want to be—with him.

From the moment Nick died, there I was, plunged into the midst of all that, and like an automaton. Everything I was programmed to do I tried my best to do. In a new place where all surety seemed to have vanished, I tried my best to *make sure*. I made sure, with a frenzy of application and anxiety, that the meals were thought through, for my family had come to be with me, and there had to be meals. I made sure that groceries were bought; that if there was not enough money in my wallet I went to the bank; that I called the lawyer; that I answered, punctiliously, the greatly appreciated condolence notes; that the lawn got mowed; that the oil was changed in the car; that bills were paid promptly; trying all the time to grasp the mathematics of the financial machine that supplied the money to keep everything running, always Nick's role.

But my stunned and fragmented mind couldn't do any of this right. Everything I tried to do was farcically incomplete or absolutely wrong. My center had been struck; what held me together had been fractionated into urgent directives, like busy, quivering, red-hot wires, all of which, independent of one another, were shrieking, "Do it, do it right!" I was drowning in tears that came with every mention of Nick; that is all there was in my center, where what mattered most was going on. Grief poured into that black hole, and grief was the best and only thing that I wanted, that should be in me, and that lay beneath the frenzy of mindlessly obedient activity clattering around it.

But gradually, day by day, week by week, the overwroughtness began to subside.

One morning I suddenly realized that for the first time, I had had a real thought. There it was, bold, clear, stepping up out of chaos, shaking off debris, standing alone and confident and unhampered: "I must not expect so much so soon," the thought spoke. "I must not expect that my entire future has to be decided right now: Should I sell one of the cars, and if so which one, for now I do not need two cars? Do I need an accountant to help me balance my checkbook? What should the memorial service be, and when?" Etc., etc.

"No. Let it all go," I said to myself. "Surrender. That which is for you will come of itself into your hands."

And stop whining. If a widow is fortunate enough to have sufficient property, she has no right to complain about having to manage it.

Then, one day, I noticed the pinks and the purples of the petunias in the big pots in the patio and the dark blue of lobelia that was, suddenly, as intense as emotion.

The feeling of being turned on after being extinguished for a long time is one that I had never had, since I had never before been extinguished in such a way. It came to me in one second's revelation, then slipped immediately off—a feeble feeling, almost offensive, almost unwanted, and certainly not believed in. But it had hit me.

In a few minutes, I was afraid to admit that I was being plugged into life again. I thought that it was awful for me to be able to feel, or to express, a good feeling, any feeling, about flowers. I ought to be crushed that it was me, not Nick, who was here in this patio looking at flowers.

(Survivor's guilt, this is called, and I recognized it then and there. Having a name for it helped a little. And later I had another thought: Perhaps the convention of black for mourning—black, which is negation—was designed to keep survivors in a lengthy state of proclaiming grief, shrouding blackly the natural assimilation of death that was being repressed in them by this grim, dark armor against anyone's invasion of it, or against their own escape from it.)

But aliveness had returned to me. And after that, it returned occasionally, sometimes welcomed, sometimes begrudged. Eventually it came back full time. There was a stubborn persistence to its recurrence.

October. I was sitting one evening in my corner of the loveseat by the fire, drinking my evening wine and looking out across the pond to the sea.

Sounds pleasant, doesn't it? Lucky me.

But try as I might to find pleasure in that ceremonial cocktail hour—it has always been that for me—I could not. In fact, that evening I was feeling a more than usual loneliness. And I couldn't cry out, "Help!" There was no help.

Spoiled? Self-indulgent? Was that it?

Not dealing well with loneliness can be quickened by self-indulgence, of course. But when all is said and done, loneliness is loneliness, and that's all, or mostly all, there is to it.

I knew that my loneliness was worse at this time of day, when I was sitting on one of the loveseats, with the other one, across the way, empty.

I also understood that this was the time of day when couples everywhere reunite after the day's separation and are together for some purpose.

For me, it always had the principal purpose of being a time of hope—never-failing hope—that there we were, after a long day's busyness, together and alone and free for an hour just to sit back and enjoy. The bell's rung! School's out! Now it will happen! I will be able to say to Nick what I am full of, and he will be able to do the same. Marvelously, suddenly, we will have a new recognition of each other, a discovery of ourselves we had never had.

It's somehow very sad that I was always wanting more from my life with Nick. I think that puts me in the category of women who, longing for what is next to impossible, have the unrealistic expectations that marriage will supply everything.

Even way back when I first married Nick, I knew that something which felt absolutely indispensable to me was missing between us. Before our first trip to Europe, and on subsequent trips anywhere, I longed for an interpenetrating, all-inclusive knowing of each other. Going away with Nick and being in some foreign place with him, carefree, on vacation, had the promise of a different and perfected relationship, one in which, away from our "rut," away from our house, away from our work, two new, free, enjoying, closer people would come into being. I didn't understand then, of course, that the bond created by our house and our outer lives was among the strongest ties we had, beyond the longing of two hearts, which I called love.

So. That was what I was always looking for in the ceremonial of the evening fireside drink—a revelation to each other of who we were and a new and fuller communion because of that.

Looking back now to my longing for what I did not have with Nick, I realize, like Paul Theroux after his divorce, that the bond created by ordinary things shared, though prosaic seeming and unromantic, was a buried treasure that my heart was unaware of:

> Years later, when Alison and I were apart, instead of all the vivid memories of marriage, it seemed strange to me that my mind went back to its satisfying monotonies,

> returned again and again to revisit its most prosaic routines. I was moved more by remembering the shopping trips to the supermarket than the weekends in Paris. It was something about sharing the burden, solving the problems, performing tasks together—painting shelves or wallpapering, putting down a carpet or cleaning the attic. Not any particular voyage, but rather our bobbing at our mooring.
>
> The memories of the long hours we had spent this way moved me most because they ought to have been a kind of hardship, and yet I treasured them because they were precious in their difficulty. Taking pleasure in them was the evidence of love. The home we had made like two busy birds, taking scraps of dead grass and bits of old string and turning them into the rough symmetry of an unshakable nest. All the time we had spent in this apparently unromantic work amounted over the long term to devotion, almost to passion.[35]

These days I look at old couples sitting wordlessly together at a restaurant table, chewing, drinking, looking all around them for distraction, but scarcely ever looking at each other. I sense the complaints about each other they are keeping to themselves, wouldn't want to utter, wouldn't dare to utter. I sense their weary, weary boredom. I sense their Siamese twin–like dependency. And I want to shout to them, I want to wave my fist at them and shout, "But don't sit there so unhappily! Can't you realize you have the greatest thing you could have at this age—each other? You. Have. Each. Other. Go together and do your marketing after you leave here. Go together to the library and take out a video to watch tonight. Go home and take your little naps, cook your careful meals, wash your supper dishes together. But before you go to sleep in your single beds that are in separate rooms because he snores and you have insomnia, before you close your eyes, know, and give thanks for, your great good fortune in, quite simply, having each other."

I wish I had been more aware, while Nick was alive, of my great good fortune in the profoundly full-filling inconsequence of bobbing at our mooring; though I think in some part of me I did, as the years went on, sense the existence of this buried treasure. Although a deeper knowing of each other never developed through talk, a very deep, unuttered communion *did* develop, my basically wordless presence for Nick, his for me. Neither of us was totally alone.

As I am now.

And so I have to admit that because Nick never *expressed* any deep knowing of me, I have been partially alone in my life with him. Could I even say, basically alone? (But isn't everyone basically alone?)

If this is so, and I am now both innately and tangibly alone, which of course I am, then I must look at loneliness in a new way. I must understand and honor the *innate* component of my loneliness, which ought to teach me not to heap all the blame of it on the absence of Nick.

And next, I must accept as irreversible the loneliness caused by the disappearance of the sustaining presence of the person I was closest to in the world—in one sense the closeness of male and female union, in another sense of friendship and of mutual dependencies. A woman who has lost a man is in an ancient condition of being left alone. And I am not exempt from it.

Understand the dualism of my loneliness. Understand the layers of it. Accept it. Don't sit in my corner of the loveseat gazing out to sea and bemoan it. School myself to be with the condition, the reality of aloneness. Rather than saying to myself, "I am lonely. I hate being lonely. This must change"; rather than sitting here with a glass of wine in my hand and bemoaning loneliness (which I am, of course, compounding, enlarging, dramatizing, by bemoaning); rather than feeling sorry for myself; rather than thinking, "this should not be happening to me," I could at the very least think about something else—about the entirety of the present moment, for instance, which is composed of the ancient essential aloneness of my nature, as well as the new tangible aloneness of the loss of Nick. If loneliness is a condition of life that I have entered into irreversibly, then at least I should accept the reality of it and try to be "the bird in the cage" singing not of joy but simply of a kind of intactness—something, as I said before, not sensation-al, something sensibly and reliably entrenched that I can believe is the best and the only source of peace.

And above all, I warned myself, don't fall into the getting-nowhere habit of thinking, "this can't happen to me."

It has happened to me.

I am alone.

If I must think about it, try perhaps to think of what else is going on that is good, if, of course, at the moment, something of value is going on.

But if not, find a strawberry.

And in a way, after that, I did. That was one of those moments when knowing and doing come together in an open and conclusive way. Throughout myself, I knew with clear composure and acceptance, was suddenly freed to know, that "it could happen to me," contrary to the motto on the little jug Nick had given me, "Don't worry, it may never happen."

Did the book do this? Did all the complexities of exploration I had been involved in for almost three years bring this about?

First, I must say that for me, or for anyone, to claim reformation or conversion has always seemed a questionable and sometimes even wishful-thinking posture. And in my case, how can I be sure that the capacity to surmount tragedy with some durability was not already there in me, only waiting to be brought to life by crisis? Or whether it was the outcome of new effort? Or a combination of both?

On the other hand, I sense that I have been altered. I *feel* different to myself. A sort of grim forbearance is a very different feeling from the youthful, mindless exuberance I remember as being my usual disposition. Resignation—a rather settled feeling, unexciting—is a different state from the charged, childlike, constant expectation that everything will turn out to be for the best in this best of all possible worlds.

And so my assumption is that some modification of my old self has gone on, that a sobering of disposition has, in effect, come about through naïve childishness tempered in some degree by a slow but steady invasion of adulthood.

My belief—which is wary and not an ironclad claim—is that without the base of the book, I mean without the groundwork of the months of exploration and occasional insight, I would not have been able to reassemble myself in the limited way I did after Nick's death. I believe, again warily, that a many-layered attentiveness to my inner and outer existence, including the very new use of thought, has, during all the months of writing this book, been contributing to more stability and to some improvement in attitude and conduct. But even long before Nick died, and even before I began this book, I think that I was always at work on some level, preparing myself for just such a fearful occurrence—with fantasies of the worst, yes, which were no fit preparation, as I knew they wouldn't be—but realistically, with the fortification of putting my mind to my life.

Conscious behavior may have contributed to an unconscious coming to grips with the disaster that struck me, but never in a way I could actually feel. For instance, I didn't lie in my bed after waking up in the morning, trying to summon up words with which to face the day. I didn't say to myself, so that I actually heard a voice in my mind, "Bear this. Deal with this. Don't fall apart. Keep on." Mindless from shock, I couldn't possibly have thought to say to myself, "*Be* the suffering."

On the surface, there was a summoning of willful recognition that the world still existed and that people I loved were around me and that I had to do what I had to do. But whatever directives I had, I did not feel them working in me.

Anyway, the book, in being one of the forces that worked for me in this crisis, did, I know, truly help me through it.

Had I learned anything from the book *before* Nick's death? Was some grown-up-ness beginning to manifest itself even before the terrible testing ground of that loss? Was it, from the writing of the book, already in the making?

Yes. I remember, through the way I sometimes dispensed

with fantasy fears and through the discoveries I made as I wrote, and also through the way I coped with Nick's illnesses, that what in hindsight I could call grown-up-ness was sporadically, and in a small way, beginning to make its appearance.

I can't possibly assess how *much* the superimposition of Nick's death on advances in myself prior to it was responsible for the way I am now. There is no possible way of knowing how much the work on the book, and how much the actual experience of crisis, separately and together, created this beginning alteration. All I know is that both the thinking experience and the event of his death are inseparable.

Also, consciously, as well as throughout myself, I know that I have a small but intermittent confidence I did not have, and one I never thought to have. Or perhaps would not really have wanted?

I'm not sure I like the feeling. Perhaps because such a small beginning strength as I have gotten makes me feel too much like a grown-up. And being grown-up *feels* like what in truth it is—being on one's own. Remaining a child feels safer, feels like the promise of being taken care of. It appears that being grown-up feels lonely and bleak; it's all up to just me now. There's no one to watch over me!

Nevertheless, like it or not, I've grown a stronger spine. And I dare to think that some small strength has come to stay, even though I do not like this life of strength.

One change, which I can confidently claim to be a result of my advocacy, in the book, of "thinking," is that I can, when I want to, think. When I am finally driven to do so because emotion is not serving me, I can put my mind where it should be in that circumstance.

The catalyst for this was Nick's death, though the training for it had been going on from the beginning of the work on this book. But his death brought me face-to-face with the challenge of having to think in ways I never had, and with a reluctant discipline that was new to me, in order to deal, alone, with the management of all the seemingly endless material details of my new existence.

Nothing will ever make me like it. I never wanted to be a businesswoman, never could have successfully been one. In fact, I rebel in every fiber of my being against this life of endless paperwork, which I do so inefficiently, digging my heels in like a crazed mule, and with a constant, lamenting resistance to the way my new clerical duties eat up my days and anxiously keep me awake at night, allowing so little time for my own work—writing—so little emotional leisure for recognition of sunsets. I can just hear my parents saying, "We all have to do things in this life we don't like, Margaret." Well, yes, I know that. Because the cry of "I want" is a child's cry. And I do see that it is essential to run my life as best I can, that *I* have to do it, no one else can, and that in a muddled, slow fashion, I *can* do it. I don't have any sense of pride in being able to do a man's job, so-called; I don't need reassurance that I can be a capable businesswoman—don't need that and don't want it. But I can see that this new full-time job of mine is one way in which I, the child, am learning that I can't continue to be cosseted and protected, and that, in settling into an acceptance of the inevitable, I am stitching myself together to run my own house and my own life, alone.

My discovery and acceptance of the fact that "it can happen to me" is one of the most important truths I have ever in my life learned. (Could this mean, I wonder, that self-concern has diminished?)

I have explained that I believed myself to be self-concerned because when things went against me, things both large and small, it simply felt impossible, even inappropriate, that this should be happening to *me*, who should be exempt from adversity, protected from it.

But through exploration and through bereavement, I found out slowly and painfully that I was not exempt from adversity, that adversity *could* happen to me because it *had* happened to me. I grew to realize, and even to accept with a certain tired relief, the reality of my equal membership in the human race. I no longer see myself as more special than other women, no longer classify myself as "chosen." I have been disrobed of that disguise, and now—undisguised, as it were—I stand along with every other woman in the world who is old and widowed and lonely. I have not been spared.

I don't know when I first began to be aware of being in a state of feeling sorry for myself and to call it self-pity; or when I realized that I had begun to have a sense of myself as being cheerlessly altered. It was as though, from the shocks and sorrows of losing my husband, I was in the process of creating for myself a new identity—that of "pitiable old widow." I was not wearing the black of widow's weeds, but I could just as well have been, from the way I felt and the way I saw myself.

And so I recognized that my initial clean, inevitable sorrow was now often shadowed by a heavy, soap-opera sensation of seeing myself alone and sad and overworked and old and so forth; thinking that old age was pitiful, was nature's bad planning, and that I was being victimized by something omnipotent and irreversible and cruel.

When one of those soap-opera moods would suddenly be clear to me, I would try very hard to get over it, and often did; and then, would, more often than not, settle into a sort of grim composure, metaphorically shrugging my shoulders in acceptance of the underlying new fact of my existence—widowhood.

That disciplinary resignation did seem to work, in its fashion, to relieve the stupor of self-pity, but I was never certain that it had real staying power. I've no doubt that the increasing habit of not letting myself get away with self-pity accrued in me, however, and made it easier, as time went on, not to wallow. As they say, every little thing helps.

But then, miraculously, I found an additional, deeper, more lasting way to deal with feeling sorry for myself. It was shown to me dramatically one morning in the kitchen as I was getting ready to squeeze orange juice for my breakfast.

I had just finished setting the table—one willowware cup and saucer, one willowware cereal bowl, one spoon, one paper napkin—when suddenly I saw this "one" of everything, including one old woman in a blue bathrobe. And for a second I was standing off from myself and viewing a scene, as though I were outside looking in through the window at this kitchen and this one old woman and her one cup and saucer and cereal bowl and spoon and paper napkin.

I stood absolutely still. I heard the silence. I heard the old clock tick, tick. I heard the faucet drip.

Pathos, I thought. That was the name of this. I was looking at the pathos of my life.

I stood and looked at the conditions of the widow I am, and I saw pathos. I saw pathos in its totality, I saw it in its menace. And I said to myself, not out loud, but in such a declarative inner way that the words still ring in my ears, "This is a pathetic sight—an old woman in her bathrobe in an empty kitchen, about to go through the motions of squeezing orange juice for herself alone. No longer does she squeeze two oranges for two glasses of juice as she did every morning up until the day her husband died. Oh no. Now every morning she squeezes one orange for one glass of juice. There is only one of everything here on this breakfast table where once there were two of everything. How soundlessly, joylessly mechanical she is, like a robot, how habitually conscientious she is—step one, step two, step three—the same schedule every morning, never a variation. Because it matters to make sure. Making sure is a necessity for an old woman who lives alone."

I saw myself doing all this. And then, as instantaneous, as clear and as vivid as a zigzag of lightning, I *saw* myself *seeing* my doing of it as the "*pitiful, voiceless habit of a lonely old widow.*"

In that second, I was detached from this woman in such a total way that she was like a life-size cardboard cutout—one-dimensional and the color blue—propped up against the kitchen counter like a department store window display.

All this went through my head in less than a second.

But then, right away, and just as clearly as I had seen the pathos of this scene and declared it to myself, I thought, "This is the way an old widow looks to the world. I am seeing this as pitiable because I *think* this is the way an old widow *appears* to the world."

I was absolutely certain of this. And the certainty hasn't left me once since I felt it. Almost immediately afterward, the thought came to me that if I took away the name I had given the scene, the name other people would give it, "pathos," what then? If I took away pity, what did I see? If I took away a verdict of "pitiable, alone widow," of some classification that had made me regard myself as doomed to a cut-and-dried aridity of silent, solitary mechanical activity within this kitchen every morning for the rest of my life—in short, if I removed an "idea" of myself from the scene of how I, how all old widows, *appear*—did this change the scene in any way?

And I saw that it did, absolutely. Even though I could see and feel that of course I was a lone woman, and that I was behaving in a silent, mechanical way, and that the "one" of everything had come to stay and that, yes, there was of course poignancy and sadness in having no one to belong to, and that it was a reality that now the hill went down instead of up and that this condition was not only universally classified as "decline" but of course was just that, nevertheless, when I stopped calling this condition "pathetic," it ceased in that moment to feel pathetic. My melancholy attitude about myself vanished, and I felt immediately and subtly better.

I saw this with sureness. I saw that I had been trapped in a cliché. I saw that my self-pity was an *attitude* I had grown to adopt as irreversible fact, and I felt how immensely limiting it was, how it shrank me, how it allowed for no other attitude but its own, and in so doing cast me in a mold in which I could become set and unchangeable. There was no latitude in it, no allowance for the continual mutability of life and of my living it. No allowance at all for change or growth.

And so I came back again to that basic parable: to suspend judgment is to see what is here. "Thinking" about being a certain way is not the reality of "being" that way. The actual *being* of a widow in a kitchen getting her breakfast and an *attitude* of being a "pathetic widow in a kitchen getting her lonely breakfast" are two separate, adversarial existences.

I had a sudden inkling of something new in myself that I could allow, and I thought: What if I stop calling my situation names?

What then?

Along the way I have discovered something that I can feel sincerely relieved and optimistic about (even though grown-up-ness can often feel so, well, drab), which is that pulling myself together has become far easier on me than giving up. Specifically, it is an easier experience to restrain emotions than it is to be torn apart by them.

Perhaps I came to this conclusion in part by learning about self-pity.

I came to the conclusion, too, one day, that the sight of the worn-out stag and doe had gotten to be depressing. The stag, in fact, had toppled over and lay with his proud head resting across the back of the doe, who was still standing, even in her blowsy disarray.

But what to do with them? I wouldn't want to burn them, I wouldn't want to drown them in the pond; I wouldn't, oh indeed I wouldn't want to bury them; and naturally, I wouldn't want to throw them on the pile of brush to be taken away and churned up into chips.

In the thicket in the field behind the house, near the brook where watercress grows, there is a little clearing. I found it by looking for it. When I saw it, I knew right away that it was the perfect, the most decent, of resting places.

And so there I put them, the stag and the doe, lying on the ground facing each other with their forelegs intertwined. And there they will be, this inseparable pair, until natural causes bring about their disintegration and, ultimately, their disappearance.

There is still one immense, blank, unexplored space in me; I do not yet know what the central intent of my life is going to be without the use of it for a man.

As I've said, my living, my existence, from the beginning of my life has been shaped by this vital principle: to live with a man, to love him, and to take care of him.

And so, for the years in my father's house, and for the years of my marriage to Sam and then for the long years of my marriage to Nick, my life has been defined by my allegiance to one man.

But now, at last, I am without a man. And I expect to remain in this inconceivable circumstance for the rest of my life.

I know this at last thoroughly, and I know it with panic, even though, at the same time, I know what a great wrong it is to allow one's life to be defined by a relationship.

In the very beginning of this book, as I was starting out to question fear, I found that I was afraid of being without my husband. I was afraid, of course, quite naturally, of being without my loving of Nick, which was the first purpose of my heart. But I was also afraid of being the little girl with no one to watch over her. And I was also, in some part of me, afraid of being left with no one to watch over—a widow with empty hands.

So now, having become that widow, the first question I must ask myself is: What am I, without a man? An Arab proverb says, "The woman without a husband is like a bird with one wing."

And the big, scary question (a question asked by thousands of aging widows, and surely the cause of one of their deepest fears): Can I *be*, without a man? I've found out that I can *survive* without Nick, but can I *be*, without him?

Is it possible for me to *be* a woman not indivisible from a man?

Can I ever become a comfortable entity?

Even as I ask that question, I remind myself that one of the two most powerful elements of my self has been my longing to have a life not defined by a Laocoön-like intertwining with a man. The desire not to be taken care of by a man has been as strong as my desire to be child to a father. The "I" of me, the thing I have kept buried and inactive and hushed up, is the thinking "I," and it is, per se, independent of any other person. It gives expression to itself and to others through definition of *itself*, not through a relationship.

But. And this is a large BUT. As it is now almost a year since Nick died, I have become independent for the first time in my life. I am freer in many ways than I have ever been. I am more resourceful, more humble about my fate. And all this adds up, I suppose, to a newfound confidence, or perhaps another word would be "security."

Then why does my life feel so low-key, so pallid, so compartmentalized? All the compartments—independence, resourcefulness, etc.—are gratefully acknowledged as steps forward, and useful, for how can I not be grateful for growth? Yet these compartments are freelancing, without a basic unifying theme to bind them together; all of them are variations, but not, as in a symphony, variations on a central theme.

It is this unboundness that makes me feel not whole, as though my marriage was a substance that bound everything in my life together and gave it meaning and purpose. This makes me feel that in spite of having achieved to some degree what I always thought would be the ultimate liberation—to function independently of a man—I am missing something so vital to happiness that the only way I can describe the feeling is to say that I am like a woman who has had—what?—a lobotomy? Or has had siphoned out of her some essential chemical? Or has been bled of her own blood and transfused with someone else's blood? The density and outlines of my whole self—body and spirit—feel this emptiness.

After so many years of using for one man that mysterious energizer I call, for want of a better word, love, I now know that love has gone far beyond any definition of it, if indeed it even began as such an abstraction. Instead, it has become a development of a part of myself that utterly needs use and expression, as a body needs air and so breathes.

Can I be happy without it?

Can I be happy without the transfusing mystery of my existence: being a woman in love, purely, with the body and soul of a man?

I knew the answer yesterday, when I put my face into the first fully flowered lilac of May, the first time I had dared to do this. Every day, fearfully, I had been passing the lilacs by. But finally I was impelled to confront a lilac. I thrust my nose deep into the cool, perfumed steeple. And here was this emotion!

I have never been able to know why it is so unfathomably wonderful to smell a lilac—until yesterday. All day I was helpless with longing, without what lilacs could bring, which was what Nick could bring—the same thing. I knew that I was parted forever from the deepest meaning of lilacs.

So the answer is no, I do not believe I can be happy, as I have known happiness, if the first purpose of my heart has no way of going on.

To sum this all up: In struggling to develop my widow's might, I will have to focus, in my solution seeking, on whatever power I can find in myself to live without the part of me that needs man and woman love purely and, too, without the part of me that distorts it with a child's need.

I will instead have to try to live *with* all the rest of me that I hope has ways (already set in motion) of eventually giving me some sort of freedom. I can only hope that I will get used to that seemingly contradictory state of being. But even if I do not, I pray for the common sense to consolidate my gains and to make the most of them.

And perhaps I will. Except in the spring, when I smell a lilac.

* * *

I make muffins (one of which, hot, I will have soon for breakfast) with more pecans and raisins from the health food store than the recipe calls for and twelve-grain organic flour and four egg whites instead of two whole eggs. I set the timer, go outdoors into the scented, still, overcast morning, sounding with surf not far off, to pick mint from my herb garden, wherein is a tall green abundance of basil, tarragon, Italian parsley, chives, and low-spreading marjoram, oregano, thyme. I linger with this greenness of aromatic delight for a moment in the soft, quiet, surf-surging fog, then go back into the kitchen and put the mint into the pleasure of an absolutely white thin teacup, strike at it with the edge of a spoon to crush it—"Mint gives out its best aroma when crushed, like a woman's heart when bruised," was part of a recipe for mint juleps that Nick and I had derisively recited in this kitchen for years and which, indeed, has become to me the look of mint, the smell of mint, the taste of mint, inseparable from that despicable southern colonel's words. I pour hot water over the mint into the white cup, carry the cup—unsteadily, damn it—out to the deck and set it down on the driftwood table Nick made. I sit down in the soft, gray silence. I close my eyes. A mockingbird's melodious racket comes from the thickness of the great cedar by the stone wall.

Afterword

SUMMER IS here for the third time since I first sat down in my tent to begin to think and to write about the fears of old age. The beach plum blossoms are past their prime—a fuzzy, pinkish cloud, no longer clearly defined beach plum flowers but only a blurred reminder of them. Lilacs are fading into a gray lavender neuterness splotched with brown, so sadly almost deceased. Beach plum, lilac, dogwood, all are in the new country of old age, becoming something unbeautifully other than what they were.

Soon, in the fields and over stone walls and white picket fences, June's roses will be here, and then all the gaudy, bursting colors of summertime. And what progress have I made since the roses of three years ago?

Well, I know that I have made some progress. Little by little, with a two steps forward and one step backward kind of advance, I have found in this foreign country a kind of terrain that seems native to it, since it keeps repeating itself at intervals like patches of dry ground in a swamp, which, when found, are predictably solid under one's feet. These frequent patches of dry ground keep me going forward in a knowledge that some safe land does reliably exist here and that I can count on it. It is bleak land, to be sure, these dry patches, and still foreign, always reminding me that life is a series of surprises and that at any moment I can arrive at the brink of something that cannot be walked upon. Still, I hope by now that I know the folly of trying to imagine what or when that might be.

And more important to me, who needs to live with joy, is the unexpected discovery that it is sometimes possible to feel the light of joy behind the darkness of sorrow—like the gold edging around a cloud that for a moment hides the sun.

I also think that it is progress, in addition to becoming more adultly capable in certain ways, to be able to say that I am not a finished old woman. This foreign country of old age has not brought me to a standstill, as I feared it might when I began this book. However, as for being exiled forever from my native country—that rubbish-heap-dom for the aged—I do know that I am, in both a minor and a major way. In a minor way I am a nonparticipant, as an aging widow can so easily be in terms of the to-dos and activities of the community I live in, though I don't care at all if this is so, because for a number of years I have, by my own choice, been outside that sort of thing anyway.

But what is really serious for me in a major way is the knowledge that I am no longer connected to the generative core of life. (And the ending of my reproductive capacity or the presence, even, of libidinous old hormones has nothing whatsoever to do with it.) It is the knowledge that I have become peripheral to the magnetized-to-one-another majority made up of those who, in primal need, belong essentially to one person. It is my recognition of the basic generalized ending, for me, of female connected to male that makes me a stranger to all that. I took a walk on Lucy Vincent Beach last week and found this out.

There was a young couple sitting entwined on the sand, with a bottle of wine between their feet. There was a young mother and father with a baby in a backpack seat jolting wonder-eyed above the father's head. There was a huge beach picnic of middle-aged men and women with coolers and barbecues and beach umbrellas and a transistor radio drowning out the sound of gulls and surf.

And then there was an old couple walking briskly together with the dogged fervor of exhausted exercisers. Their faces were alive and contented, and they were holding hands.

So it was that as I walked along the edge of the sea by myself I understood quite suddenly and absolutely that I was an outsider.

It wasn't, though, that I had wanted to be that girl entwined with that boy, drinking wine. Or that I longed to be the wife of that man carrying their baby on his back.

No. What I did want with all my being was to be that old woman walking breathlessly along beside the old man whose hand she was holding with such devotion.

If I had been that woman, holding with love the hand of a man, I would not, in spite of the abundance of connected life on this beach, have felt outside of it.

And so, yes, and with a set jaw I know it: I *am*, *indeed*, peripheral.

But still—and a set jaw isn't bad, it's reinforcing—I know that being a peripheral woman doesn't mean that I am a finished old woman, for I am not. I am an old woman growing up.

* * *

There is a reality that I am not ignoring when talking about progress, and which is important to acknowledge: there is no such thing as complete change. One can do one's best and often achieve some reform that gives more meaning or more happiness to one's life. But there is no total elimination of the suffering and the perplexities of being human, no total reversal of complex, troubled person to uncomplex, untroubled person.

What ongoingness I have is dormant for periods, alive for periods. Back and forth. Up and down. But fortunately, if aliveness goes, it invariably returns, and a part of my new confidence is knowing that it will.

There are no promises of perfection. But there is faith—in the life-saving instinct not to stand still, which keeps one going and going, and in the life-giving hope that *some* release from being a complex, troubled person is possible if one keeps on trying for it.

There can be progress forward. That is the kind of progress I think I have made since the roses of three years ago. And that is all I am claiming for myself.

There is no conscious or purposeful way to produce a moment of insight, nor any way at all, consciously, to make it stay. What it does, it does quickly. It comes, it goes. But though it flashes out almost as soon as it has flashed in, it leaves its message, which is fed back into the accumulated wisdom of the gestating gestalt, never to be lost.

Coming on a particular day at a particular moment, insight derives not from that day or that moment but from a whole lifetime of days and moments that have coalesced, meshed, for a second, into a perfect, clear statement of the true nature of whatever it is that the insight is about. For that one rare second, on that particular day, triggered by I do not know what, the conditions are exactly right for a coming together—with an illuminatingly summarizing explanation—of all the elements of one's living that have had a bearing on a particular issue.

So it was one day shortly before Nick died. I was sitting with him at the kitchen table having lunch, in no special frame of mind that I recall, eating. Occasional talk.

I was looking through the window across the field to the pond, and beyond, to the sea.

Then, there it was. I was invaded by something unidentifiable. Immense. It had slipped in without any forewarning that I was aware of, and had suffused my consciousness. For a moment that was a second or an eternity, I knew that, sitting there, I saw, grasped, encompassed, *lived*, in a clarity I had never before experienced, the presence of everything in my life at it was at that moment, including myself in appropriate balance with it.

I believe now that what I was experiencing was both my capacity and my ability to have a oneness with existence be the ultimate verity of it. I believe that after months of attentiveness—to the world around me and to the egoism within me—I was all at once experiencing an evolved ability to be, momentarily, with and in that present moment—my self (I am), existing objectively and thus limitlessly with field, pond, sea, kitchen, my husband, my world. There was no evaluation of this or even any recognition of wonder or astonishment or curiosity. Incalculably immense, it simply was.

I was not conscious of myself, only of existence.

"Who is this ever-present 'I' that is not me?"[36]

*   *   *

But practically speaking, what is the significance of that moment of insight for my day-to-day living? And for the use of it as an ending to this book?

I interpret it, and feel it, as a disclosure. And I see its significance—to me and as a conclusion to the book—as primarily that. It did disclose to me, and should keep on reminding me that it *is* possible, even if only for a second, to be located in the entirety of the here and now; it *is* possible to be without friction and without judgment and thus to experience an objective existence that is reality.

I see that such a transcendent experience was an ultimate instruction, teaching me, once and for all, that my struggle for attentiveness has been on target and that everything but the explosion of recognizing and being in the present moment is basically peripheral to it, irrelevant to it, off there somewhere without reality.

In short, reality is now. Reality is the strawberry. And fantasy fears of old age cannot coexist with it. That is the essential message of this book.

The importance, too, of that moment of insight is the revelation of the limitless capacity of a human being to ascend toward his betterment. It is a reminder to keep the infinite possibilities of himself in mind. To aspire toward a deemphasizing of himself and toward the courage and the common sense to take what comes. Like a guiding star in the sky, the knowledge of the possibility of insights reminds him to put forth his strength.

And so at the end of this book that has been a search to find the meaning of the fear of old age and a solution to the lessening of it, I ask myself, "Where is fear now?"

And I answer, "Fear is where I let it be."

Notes

1. Dr. Margaret Brenman-Gibson, personal communication.
2. T. S. Eliot, *Four Quartets: East Coker*.
3. George Mills, "Autumn Swans," in *The House Sails out of Sight of Home* (Boston: Northeastern University Press, 1991), 66.
4. Dylan Thomas, "Do Not Go Gentle into That Good Night."
5. Dr. Margaret Brenman-Gibson, personal communication.
6. John Donne, "Devotions upon Emergent Occasions."
7. *Hamlet* III, iii, 40.
8. Charlotte Joko Beck, "A Parable," in *Zen Flesh, Zen Bones: A Collection of Zen and Pre-Zen Writings*, comp. Paul Reps (New York: Doubleday, 1961), as quoted in *Everyday Zen*, Charlotte Joko Beck (San Francisco: HarperCollins, 1989), 119–120.
9. Alan W. Watts, *The Wisdom of Insecurity* (New York: Pantheon, 1951), 117.
10. Marianne Moore, "Idiosyncrasy and Technique," in *A Marianne Moore Reader* (New York: Viking Press, 1961), 169.
11. Watts, *Wisdom of Insecurity*, 98.
12. Watts, *Wisdom of Insecurity*, 130.
13. Marianne Moore, "In Distrust of Merits," in *A Marianne Moore Reader*, 43.
14. Jean-Paul Sartre.
15. Jon Kabat-Zinn, *Wherever You Go, There You Are* (New York: Hyperion, 1994), 57.

16. Lyrics from "Someone to Watch over Me" by George and Ira Gershwin. Copyright © 1926 (renewed) New World Music Corp.

17. Spinoza.

18. William James, *Principles of Psychology* (Chicago: Encyclopedia Britannica, 1952).

19. Watts, *Wisdom of Insecurity*, 51.

20. John Cheever, *The Journals of John Cheever* (New York: Alfred A. Knopf, 1991), 42.

21. May Sarton, *Journal of a Solitude* (New York: W. W. Norton, 1973), 31.

22. Nyanaponika, *The Heart of Buddhist Meditation* (New York: Citadel Press, 1969), 21.

23. Nyanaponika, *Heart of Buddhist Meditation*, 23.

24. Margaret Brenman-Gibson, "Notes on the Study of Creative Progress," in *Psychology versus Metapsychology: Psychological Issues,* (New York: International Universities Press, 1976), 339, 354.

25. Alfred, Lord Tennyson.

26. Source unknown.

27. George Wilhelm Friedrich Hegel.

28. Moore, *A Marianne Moore Reader*, 65.

29. Thomas Carlyle, "Today."

30. Alfred, Lord Tennyson, "In Memoriam A. H. H."

31. Philip O'Connor, *Memoirs of a Public Baby* (New York: W. W. Norton, 1988), 229.

32. Watts, *Wisdom of Insecurity*, 124.

33. *Romeo and Juliet* II, ii, 50.

34. *Merriam Webster's Collegiate Dictionary*, 10th ed., s.v. "revolution."

35. Paul Theroux, *My Other Life* (Boston: Houghton Mifflin, 1996), 427.

36. Peter Matthiessen, *The Snow Leopard* (New York: Viking Press, 1978), 136.

Acknowledgments

I AM grateful beyond words to Peter Jennison for his interest, encouragement and imagination in helping me bring this book to its conclusion. And I can never thank Bliss and Gitta Carnochan enough for their lovely generosity in giving me invaluable editorial criticism in the early stages of the book. I want, too, to thank Donna Bouchard, who typed revision after revision of parts of the manuscript so flawlessly and uncomplainingly.